Paul

&

The Mysteries

Of God

The Secrets of God are
Mountain Peaks of Truth
Sustaining the Child of God

(A Pastoral Commentary and Study of Paul's Life
and Jesus' Post-Resurrection Teaching of Paul)

William L. Owens

Paul and the Mysteries of God

All biblical references are from the *King James Version* of *The Holy Bible* quoted from Logos Bible Software.

Printed and distributed in the United States of America by Create Space — an Amazon company.

ISBN-13: 978-1539101253

ISBN-10: 1539101258

BISAC: Religion / Biblical Commentary / Bible / New Testament

Published by:

222 Plan Publications, 610 Republican Road, Clarks Hill, SC

Dedication

This commentary is dedicated
to the student scholars at
Carolina College of Biblical Studies
who are completing the vision
by *rightly dividing the Word of Truth.*

Acknowledgments

I am especially appreciative of the late Robert Gee Witty, founder and first president of Luther Rice Seminary. Dr. Witty was a mentor beyond excellence. He passed to me his high view of Scripture. He believed the Bible to be God breathed and without error in the original autographs. I share the same conviction because of the Holy Spirit's witness to my spirit that the Bible is the inspired Word of God.

Witty impacted my life by employing a teaching method he discovered while studying for his Ph.D. in rhetoric at the University of Florida. He used the strategy when developing the curriculum at Luther Rice Seminary. The system of teaching was known as inter-leafing, initiated and developed by Issac Watts. Dr. Watts used his unique procedure to teach theological students under his tutelage.

I am appreciative of those friends God has brought into my life. They have encouraged me and offered useful counsel. The Lord has also given me others who have assisted me in proofing this book. I am particularly indebted to Dr. Joe Duerr, Sue Daniels and Diane Casey for aiding me in discovering my grammatical deficiencies. Their aid was enormously helpful. My pastor Dr. Bob Whaley read the manuscript and offered his insight and encouragement. My friends and fellow pastors, Jerry Wilson, Richard Daniels, and Lance Thomas read the book acting as my theological sounding board.

Thank you one and all for your labor of love in promoting the study of God's Word. It took you all to make this a successful project. My Judy deserves a special thank you. She encouraged and chided me in proper doses at just the right time.

Table of Contents

Foreword

By Bill F. Korver, D. Min.

I have the great privilege of serving Jesus Christ vocationally. It has been my joy to do so for the past 35 years. Since 2004 I have been able to do so at Carolina College of Biblical Studies (CCBS). I mention CCBS because it is a ministry founded, in 1973, as the result of Dr. William L. "Bill" Owens' visionary leadership. Resulting from his obedience to God's prompting, more than 6,000 men and women have received biblical higher education. If Owens had not stepped out in obedience and faith, I would probably not be doing what I have been the past thirteen years or more.

Besides Dr. Owens' obedience to God, I admire many other traits about him, they include but are not limited to the following: His unfailing commitment to honor Jesus Christ, the Lord of the church. It is evident in this volume as well as others he has written and in personal conversation with him. I also love his tenacious commitment to the inerrancy of Scripture, the Bible. Like me, Owens believes that it is the infallible revelation of God to man that can and should be trusted completely. I further admire Owens' long-term practice of discipling others personally and through his writing ministry. He's been doing both for five decades and the body of Christ is the better for it! Lastly, I admire that though Owens would now qualify as a "senior citizen", like Caleb of the Old Testament he is eager to tackle new projects, scale new mountains for the glory of our King, Jesus.

It takes a great deal of discipline to write a book that is both thoughtful and doctrinally sound, I'm so thankful Bill was disciplined enough to create this resource.

In this volume Owens demonstrates his giftedness as an interpreter of scripture as he provides his readers with an excellent summary of the conversion and subsequent ministry of Saul, who became the apostle Paul. What a loving and great God, who graciously calls rebels like Saul, who hated Christians and Jesus, justifies them by their faith alone and then gloriously uses them!

As you will discover in this volume, Paul was used by God to record nearly one half of the books of the New Testament. As he wrote these books God's Spirit not only directed him what to write (2 Peter 1:21) but also gave him new truths (progressive revelation). These mysteries - truths not previously known to men and unknowable by men except for God's revelation but presently (first century) revealed to man by God (Ephesians 3:4-6) – are the subject of the latter part of the volume.

I am confident that this volume will be a great resource to all who read it. I highly commend my predecessor and co-laborer for Christ, William L. Owens', efforts to produce such a work that highlights one of the choicest servants of Jesus Christ, Paul the apostle, and many of the mysteries he was privileged to record for our profit.

Bill F. Korver, D. Min., President,
Carolina College of Biblical Studies,
Fayetteville, North Carolina

Introduction

(To be read)

The motivation for this book comes from studying the life of our Lord and His relationship to His apostles. His particular and unique message to them drew me to study its content at various junctures of His ministry. When closely observed, I discerned that His pre-crucifixion ministry was almost exclusively Jewish in nature. He occasionally ministered to Gentiles, but His focus was on the nation of Israel. He presented Himself as Israel's eagerly anticipated Messiah. On numerous occasions, Israel's religious and political leadership rejected Him. Why? Because, they ultimately did not believe His claim that God was His Father.

Israel's spiritual eyes were blinded by their preconceived notions that their Messiah could and would only come as a political deliverer from the enslavement of a foreign nation and would set Himself up as their King. They were contemplating deliverance from Roman bondage by one analogous to Moses as he delivered Israel from the bondage of Egypt.

The emphasis of the message changed as God's focus shifted from Israel to the Gentiles. The basis for God's Word has always been mercy and grace to those who placed their faith in His witness. But, as He redirected His attention to the Gentiles, God plainly revealed to Paul (who is the apostle to the Gentiles) how His new people (the Church) would come to Him and what blessings would be their's as they lived placing their faith in His witness. What

Jesus taught Paul is God's witness to all mankind.[1] All who believe will be saved and blessed.

Note the following basic parameters and presupposed observations before reading *Paul and the Mysteries of God*.

The volume is in two major parts; the first is an expositional summary of the life and mission activities of Paul the apostle; the second is an exposition of key mysteries Jesus taught Paul in his Arabian retreat. The mysteries are not dealt with exhaustively. I have chosen to be selective and provide instruction concerning the ones that are critical to understanding the overall message of the Bible relating to Paul's mission. In the appendixes I have provided a chronological list of the passages in which the mysteries are mentioned.

I believe the Bible was written by inspired men chosen of God who received their inspiration only from the Holy Spirit (2 Peter 1:20, 21). These men did not receive their inspiration as *dictation*, but rather, He moved upon their spirit and He used their personality while precisely communicating the Word of the Father. Therefore as they were moved they wrote.

I view the Bible as having no error in the original manuscripts. I also recognize we no longer have those original documents. However, we do have copies from ancient scribes providing us assurance of accuracy. Why? Because language scholars comparing these fragments are able with a high degree of accuracy to reconstruct the original. In this manner, biblical criticism provides us with assurance and confidence showing us that the most

---

[1] For a fuller discussion of Jesus' teaching, see *What Jesus Taught* by William L. Owens.

questioned passages do not affect the accuracy of the Bible's message or teaching.

I further believe the Holy Spirit has preserved the doctrinal integrity of the various translations into other languages. For example, when we hold in our hands a particular Bible translation, we have God's essential message clearly presented for our benefit and His glory.[2]

As Christians, we are privileged beyond measure! Why? Because, most Christians have available a personal copy of God's Word translated in their own language. This has only been possible for about four hundred years.

In the times of Jesus, and the prophets before Him, only the Jewish scribes and rabbis had access to Old Testament scrolls. The people of God had to depend on their rabbis and prophets to understand the way of God.

These early letters circulated from the apostles and Luke (the physician) became part of the final compilation of books we call The New Testament. These letters were not available in wide distribution. Sharing the contents with other congregations came by circulating handwritten copies. Much time would pass before these documents would become a complete library of books forming The Holy Bible, composed of both Old and New Testaments.

One astounding fact promotes The Holy Bible as uniquely the Word of God. The world-class theologian Charles C. Ryrie wrote of it in his Survey of the Bible. He said: *It was written over a period of*

---

[2] The only exception to this statement would be translations made by denominations that do not subscribe to orthodox Christianity.

approximately 1500 years by 40 different authors, and yet it is one book without contradiction in what it says.[3] Any student challenging the Bible's authenticity will have to disprove Ryrie's statement about no contradictions in what the text says.[4]

I am of the opinion that with the coming of the Lord, we will observe that true science and the Bible will be in perfect harmony. Why? Because God is the originator of both!

It would be approximately another thousand years before these Scriptures, Old and New Testaments, would be available beyond the walls of monasteries and places of higher learning where scribes carefully made copies of the original documents. The Scriptures would still be in limited supply until the invention of the printing press some time around 1,450 AD. Making the Bible available to everyone has been a painfully slow process, but the reality is finally here for most of the world's population.

Paul and his fellow scholars were privileged to have had access to copies of the Old Testament. Many probably thought God had completed His revelation. Why? There had been no prophetic word from an affirmed prophet of God for more than four hundred years. Little did they know that the last prophet would be God's only begotten Son (John 1:18).

---

[3] A Survey of the Bible, Charles C. Ryrie, Chicago: Moody Press, 1972

[4] While many have claimed the Bible is full of contradictions, no one has proven their claims except to the satisfaction of those scholars whose presupposition is that God does not exist. To open-minded scholars, there are clear academic explanations for claims of contradictions. More claims disappear with increasing numbers of archeological discoveries.

Paul and his fellow students, studying in Jerusalem's eminently touted rabbinical school, were privileged to have had access to the written Word when they gathered for studies under their teacher's guidance. We have limited insight into the methods of the rabbinical school, but we can say with certainty that students did not have the exhaustive research tools available to us in our century. But, what they did have was an accurate system of study based on a language natively used and an understanding of the culture that today's student is constantly trying to recapture.

We know they used a precise scribal system for duplicating Scripture. They possessed vast stores of historical records providing them with accurate cultural background. The laws of the rabbis were meticulously developed from Old Testament exegesis. However, the damaging negative was that the Truth was filtered through their human traditions. Jesus was very critical of their traditions because they often mixed Truth with error (Matthew 15:3, 6).

The Jewish expectation during the Second Temple period concerning the coming Messiah was nationalistic in scope. The Jewish view of the Messiah's arrival was about saving their nation from the tyranny of foreign powers. They expected a Messiah who would restore Israel to the glory years of David and Solomon. Most people had lost their hope. Let me remind you again that there had been a period of about four hundred years of silence without a word from God. No prophet had spoken!

Jehovah was true to His promise! He promised a redeemer and He sent His Son (Galatians 4:4). The story of man's awareness of Jesus' identity as the Son of God began with Elizabeth (the mother of

John the Baptist). She had a moment of realization when, upon a visit from the virgin mother, Mary, John leaped in her womb. God opened Elizabeth's spiritual eyes and she realized Mary was carrying God's promised Messiah.

After Jesus's birth, Mary and Joseph brought Jesus to the temple for His circumcision. At the temple was a man named Simeon. We are not told why he was there. It is reasonable to assume he was waiting to worship or participate in daily meditations and ceremonial cleansing. It was a divine appointment. He was a man whom God had promised would not die until he had seen the Lord's salvation. Upon seeing Mary and Joseph with Jesus, he took the baby in his arms and lifted his eyes in worship. He had immediately recognized the fulfillment of the Father's promise (Luke 2:25-32).

Again, some thirty years later, John was preaching. He exhorted Israel by declaring the nation needed to prepare ...*the way of the Lord.* The next day he was moved by the Holy Spirit when he saw Jesus and he declared, . . . *Behold the Lamb of God who takes away the sin of the world* (John 1:29).

The last Word mankind has received from God has come through Jesus Christ the Son of God. The Lord Jesus lived a sinless life and taught His disciples what His Father is like. With His sermon on the mount, Christ revolutionized prevalent and commonly held interpretations about the Laws of God. Jesus taught that what a man thought preceded his actions. Therefore, Jesus' Sermon on the Mount contradicted much of what the religious leaders had been teaching about keeping the *Laws of Moses*. The essential difference from their teaching and that of Jesus was this: Jesus focused on **the motive of the heart.**

After Jesus' baptism by John, and after His forty days and forty nights of fasting in the wilderness of Judea, Jesus faced the trial of temptation by Satan (Luke 4:1-8). Jesus came out of His trial victorious and began His public ministry to the lost sheep of the house of Israel. His Gospel was . . .*The time is fulfilled, and the kingdom of God is at hand: repent ye, and believe in the gospel* (Mark 11:15).

After Jesus' sinless life and faithful ministry He offered Himself as the sacrificial *Lamb Of God*. On the third day, He was raised by the Spirit unto a glorified supernatural body. He ministered in His resurrected body to the disciples twice in the upper room in Jerusalem (Luke 24:36), to two travelers on the Emmaus road (Luke 24:13), and again to His disciples in Galilee (Matthew 28:16-17). According to Scripture, as many as five hundred or more witnessed the resurrected Christ (1 Corinthians 15:6). Saul (whose Roman name is Paul) also saw Jesus as light on the road to Damascus and experienced a miraculous conversion (Acts 9:3-6).

Paul retired to Arabia for an extended retreat. It was here that the resurrected Jesus came to him and mentored him about *the secret things of God*. Jesus taught Paul for approximately three years (whether caught up to heaven or in a vision we do not know) (2 Corinthians 12:1-4).[5]

Being a scholar, Paul likely recorded a diary of his experience with Jesus. While we have no official

---

[5] J. Vernon McGee, in his *Thru The Bible*, is of the opinion that Paul is referencing an event in which he was stoned and left for dead but later revived.

evidence of such, he likely used instinctively his rabbinic training. Paul held in his mind and heart the teaching Jesus shared with him. Then, when the Holy Spirit had prompted, he wrote and preached. The point is this: God had given Paul an extraordinary mind with precise recall. Through the Spirit's over-sight he recorded vital teaching for the edification and work of the Church. In this manner, he completed his mission of preaching and recording God's Truth for all generations that followed. The Holy Spirit ensured Paul's letters became part of our Scriptures.

The early churches agreed that with the completion of both the Old and New Testaments, revelation from God had ceased. God is currently working through His Spirit to accomplish His primary goal of restoring His glory and transforming His people into the likeness of His Son (Philippians 3:21).

Excepting the Lord Jesus, Paul may well have been the most important person who has ever influenced western thinking. Why would this be so? Because Paul's letters form the core of Christian teaching that has largely molded Western civilization. He provided the Jewish and Gentile worlds with a new perspective on Old Testament Law. His perspective has revolutionized the thinking of those who choose to believe Jesus is the Messiah.

PART ONE

A Survey of
Paul's Life

For I am not ashamed of the gospel of Christ; for it is the power of God unto salvation to everyone that believes; to the Jew first, and also to the Greek.

Romans 1:16 (KJV)

A Brief Pastoral Commentary
on Luke's Account of Paul's Life

Chapter 1

Paul's Heritage

AD 33 (Acts 6-8)

We know virtually nothing about Saul of Tarsus outside of the biblical record. What little can be gleaned from secular records is anything but definitive. One might have made some historical discoveries referencing his family, but little with certainty. There are several references from the post-apostolic era.

For our purposes, we take all information from Scriptures, beginning with Acts and including some of Paul's letters to the churches. We believe these are the only authoritative sources of information. We begin with the first mention of Saul in Acts 7:58 and continue unfolding his story until its completion in Acts 28:31.

The Early Life

He was born in Tarsus in the region of Cilicia in southern Turkey (Acts 23:5). The date of his birth is commonly acknowledged to be from 2 to 5 AD. His parents named him Saul—likely after King Saul of Israel. It was a common name for Jewish boys of his time. His family linage was of the tribe of Benjamin (Philippians 3:5).

Tarsus was part of the Roman Empire; therefore, he was a Roman citizen. Being born in a Roman province gave him standing as a *free man,* which meant he was not destined for common servitude.

Saul's family lived in the midst of a culture that had been under Hellenistic or Greek influence. Many Jews had begun to move from a strict use of the Hebrew and Aramaic languages to the commonly spoken Greek. Saul's parents were tenacious in their adherence to the *old ways.* There is little information about his life in Tarsus not common to the era.

Paul's Religious Heritage

In all probability, both Saul's father and grandfather were Pharisees. The Pharisees were a strict Jewish sect holding to a plain or literal interpretation of Scripture. There were two other sects popular in Judaism at the time: Sadducees and Essenes. The Sadducees were more liberal in their spiritual application of the Scriptures and did not believe in an after-life nor angels. The Essenes, the third sect, were separatists, more pious and commonly lived in monastic communities. The Essenes are often connected with Qumran, a Jewish sectarian community near where the Dead Sea Scrolls were discovered. The colony was active during the time of Saul's rabbinical studies. The Essenes are described by Espinoza as, *A Jewish religious group of the Second Temple Period that emerged and flourished in Palestine from the second century BC to the first century AD.*[6] They emphasized physical and spiritual purity as they waited for the coming of the Messiah.

Raised a practicing Jew, Paul engaged in normal ceremonial cleanings, baptisms, and strict adherence to the Torah.[7] In these volumes God recorded the history of origins of all creations including the story of man's beginning.

The first parents began in innocence and ended in an act of rebellion. God, in His mercy, provided information about how He restored the first parents to His fellowship and how from the offspring of Abraham He chose Israel out of the nations to bear His name and gave them the *Laws of God.*

Paul's Education

Little is known of Saul's education in his youth. In all probability, he was trained by his

---

[6] Benjamin D. Espinoza, *Essenes*, ed. John D. Barry et al., *The Lexham Bible Dictionary* (Bellingham, WA: Lexham Press, 2016).

[7] The first five books of the Bible are called the Torah. These are the books of Moses: Genesis, Exodus, Leviticus, Numbers, and Deuteronomy.

parents to be a tent-maker thus making him vocationally independent. It was common among the Jews of this period to prepare children to earn a living for a public life. This was especially true for those who would later be groomed for what we would call a formal profession such as medicine, law, philosophy, or theological studies.

The Jews were probably brought to Tarsus by the Romans in 171 BC to promote business in the region. In this context, his parents (as mentioned above) taught him the Hebrew and Aramaic languages. He lived in a city that spoke both Greek and Latin; he likely mastered these languages as he matured in daily exchange with his neighbors.

Tarsus as a city was quite cosmopolitan. With a sea port and an adjacent trade route it commanded the attention of the Roman authorities. Sometime after the age of 12, we assume Saul went to Jerusalem for his formal training under the famous Jewish Rabbi Gamaliel. Of all rabbinic teachers in the Hillel school, Gamaliel was reportedly the most influential. The school, promoted by the Pharisaic sect, had Gamaliel's grandfather Rabbi Hillel as founder.[8]

While Saul had been completing his studies in Jerusalem, Jesus was probably beginning His ministry. It was about this time that Jesus was baptized in the Jordan by His cousin John.

Paul Persecutes Followers of Jesus

---

[8] Some have thought Paul to be a member of the Sanhedrin. However, this is unlikely because some report membership required one to be married and at least thirty years of age. Unless he had been exempted from the rules, he was not a member of the Sanhedrin. However, he was Pharisee (Philippians 3:5). He had become a Pharisee around 31 AD when he was about twenty-six. Most scholars believe he was not married.

Saul likely viewed himself as a strict rigorist among Pharisees and was a rising theological star and scholar among his fellows (Galatians 1:14; Phillipians 3:5–6). It is unclear how he gained leadership in persecuting the new sect that followed Jesus. When Luke tells the story in Acts, one clearly sees Saul as the predominant leader in the Jewish strategy to destroy the sect claiming faith in Jesus as the Messiah. His idealism exceeded that of his teacher Gamaliel—who was more tolerant in applying the traditions of a demanding faith.

Drawing our attention are two major events linked directly to Saul of Tarsus establishing him as an avowed enemy of Jesus and His followers.

The Persecution and Death of Stephen

The first of these was the stoning of Stephen, a young deacon of the Jerusalem assembly of believing Jews. Stephen had been falsely accused of preaching against Judaism and the Law of Moses. We may read the record from:

Acts 6:8-15

> *8 And Stephen, full of faith and power, did great wonders and miracles among the people.*
> *9 Then there arose certain of the synagogue, which is called the synagogue of the Libertines, and Cyrenians, and Alexandrians, and of them of Cilicia and of Asia, disputing with Stephen.*
> *10 And they were not able to resist the wisdom and the spirit by which he spake.*
> *11 Then they suborned men, which said, We have heard him speak blasphemous words against Moses, and against God.*
> *12 And they stirred up the people, and the elders, and the scribes, and came upon him,*

and caught him, and brought him to the council,
13 And set up false witnesses, which said, This man ceaseth not to speak blasphemous words against this holy place, and the law:
14 For we have heard him say, that this Jesus of Nazareth shall destroy this place, and shall change the customs which Moses delivered us.
15 And all that sat in the council, looking stedfastly on him, saw his face as it had been the face of an angel.

When Stephen had spoken, he presented a survey of God's faithful deliverance of Israel from slavery and how Scripture witnessed to Jesus' being the promised Messiah. Stephen said it was the Messiah whom the Jewish authorities schemed to have killed. He accused his hearers of being responsible for slaying God's own Son. At the conclusion of Stephen's message (recorded in Acts 7) Luke pens the following report:

Acts 7:54-60

54 When they heard these things, they were cut to the heart, and they gnashed on him with their teeth.

55 But he, being full of the Holy Ghost, looked up stedfastly into heaven, and saw the glory of God, and Jesus standing on the right hand of God,

56 And said, Behold, I see the heavens opened, and the Son of man standing on the right hand of God.
57 Then they cried out with a loud voice, and stopped their ears, and ran upon him with one accord,
58 And cast him out of the city, and stoned him: and the witnesses laid down their clothes

at a young man's feet, whose name was Saul.
59 *And they stoned Stephen, calling upon God, and saying, Lord Jesus, receive my spirit.*
60 *And he kneeled down, and cried with a loud voice, Lord, lay not this sin to their charge. And when he had said this, he fell asleep.*

Saul, willingly and some might say gleefully, participated in the stoning of Stephen. To Saul, Stephen represented a threat to all he had ever been taught. Even as Stephen gave his final witness, Saul and those who stoned him were hardened in heart and were spiritually blinded by their religious pride and did not receive God's Truth from Stephen.

The Persecution of Damascus Believers

A short time after Stephen's death, Saul appealed to the high priest to provide him with credentials that he might have authority to seek out the followers of Jesus who they believed were heretics preaching against the Law given by Moses.

Upon receiving the proper documents, Saul and an escort consisting of an undisclosed number of temple guards proceeded to Damascus. Saul had received the word from unknown sources about a sizable number of detractors who had fled to Damascus to escape the religious persecution of the believing Jews.

Saul made his arrangements, gathered his supplies, procured his escort, and set in motion his plan to put an early end to heretical members who believed Jesus was the promised Messiah. But, somewhere between Jerusalem and Damascus the entourage suddenly experienced an unexplainable light of such intensity that Saul fell to the earth.

Luke records the event in:

Acts 9:2-9

> **2** *And desired of him letters to Damascus to the synagogues, that if he found any of this way, whether they were men or women, he might bring them bound unto Jerusalem.*
> **3** *And as he journeyed, he came near Damascus: and suddenly there shined round about him a light from heaven:*
> **4** *And he fell to the earth, and heard a voice saying unto him, Saul, Saul, why persecutest thou me?*

The two major acts against Christianity led by Saul were: (1) he sanctioned the stoning of Stephen and (2) he led an attempt to arrest believers in Damascus. He had a vile contempt for those who followed Jesus. He believed with all his being that he was following the will of God in seeking their destruction. He sincerely believed Jesus' followers were heretics and needed to be eliminated for Judaism to remain pure.

Saul was a young theologian with a raging zeal for strict obedience to Truth as he understood it. By contrast, his teacher Gamaliel, was a tolerant man who was mature enough to know he may not have a correct understanding of all the Scriptures received from God. It was out of his maturity that Gamaliel told his fellow Jews to leave the believers to God's judgment. His attitude was, if they are not of God, nothing will become of them.

Saul's theological blindness reminds me of the legalists in our own day who believe all who do not view the Scripture as they do are on their way to Hell. They gleefully point to errors of others and exonerate themselves in self-righteousness.

Because of our sin nature, we all have a tendency to fall into the same trap or one like it.

Questions for Discussion

1. Why did Paul's parents likely give him the Hebrew name Saul?

2. To what Jewish sect did Paul's family belong?

3. From whom did Paul receive his formal education?

4. Describe the two cited occasions when Paul persecuted Christians.

5. What spiritual trap did Saul fall into that, if not sensitive to the Holy Spirit, believers in every generation are subject to?

Chapter 2

Paul's Conversion
And Ministry

AD 33 (Acts 9:1-19)

Paul's Conversion

Imagine Saul's shock when on the road to Damascus, he heard the master's challenge come to him from a blazingly bright light. Christ (the Lord God) identified himself as Jesus. Luke records the experience following the challenge in Acts 9:

Acts 9:5-9

> *5 And he said, Who art thou, Lord? And the Lord said, I am Jesus whom thou persecutest: it is hard for thee to kick against the pricks.*
> *6 And he trembling and astonished said, Lord, what wilt thou have me to do? And the Lord said unto him, Arise, and go into the city, and it shall be told thee what thou must do.*
> *7 And the men which journeyed with him stood speechless, hearing a voice, but seeing no man.*
> *8 And Saul arose from the earth; and when his eyes were opened, he saw no man: but they led him by the hand, and brought him into Damascus.*
> *9 And he was three days without sight, and neither did eat nor drink.*

Suddenly, Saul was stunned by the light and the voice calling out his name—asking him why he was persecuting Him. With the sound of Jesus' voice, there was instant recognition of Jesus' Lordship (Acts 9:5, 6). The capital letter in *Lord* indicates the speaker is the Lord God Almighty.

The Lord spoke in a vision to a man in Damascus named Ananias. In Ananias' vision, God told him to go to Straight Street to the house of a man named Judas and there inquire about a man named Saul of Tarsus. The Lord told Ananias Saul would be praying, and he was to lay his hands on Saul and he would receive his sight.

Ananias hesitated because of Saul's reputation as an aggressive persecutor of Christians. The Lord informed Ananias about Saul being a chosen vessel to bear the Lord's name before Gentiles, kings and the children of Israel. Ananias obeyed the Lord; he laid hands on Saul and he received his sight.

When Ananias placed his hands on Saul, he received the Holy Spirit and was baptized. He remained in Damascus spending time with local believers who had likely fled the persecution by Jews in Jerusalem (Acts 9:11-19). He even testified in the local synagogue that Christ is the Son of God. His doctrine about Christ infuriated many of the Jews. He remained in Damascus for some time—it is uncertain how long. Because of his teaching about Christ, some of the local Jews devised a plan to kill him. Saul's fellow disciples heard about the plot and aided him in his escape by letting him down in a basket over the Damascus city wall (Acts 9:20-25).

Saul's conversion was so important to the plan of God that the Holy Spirit had Luke record the experience in the Book of Acts on three separate occasions. Saul likely referenced his salvation event for two possible reasons: 1) to show he had had a real life encounter with the living Christ and 2) the incredible change to his life proved it (Acts 9:19-29; 22:1-21; 26:1-23). He would never be the *old* Saul again. Soon, after his Damascus Road experience with Jesus, Saul began to adopt the use of his Roman name Paul.

Paul's Commission

There seems to be some discrepancy among Pauline scholars about what happened after Paul fled the attempt to annihilate him in Damascus. After his conversion, Paul visited Jerusalem sometime between AD 34 and AD 35. The Jews forced him to leave because they believed he was a heretic worthy of death. He hastily returned to

Damascus and from there retreated for an extended time into Arabia as stated above. One expositor suggests that after his conversion, Paul found it necessary to retreat from public life for a season to get his thoughts around his new message. The commentator continued to say Paul was a thinker and he had to sort through how to reconcile his experience with what he had earlier believed about God.

Meditating on these comments quickly caused me to reject most of these conclusions. Why? Because, the explanations seem to suggest Paul's conversion was the result of some philosophical shift in his natural reasoning, instead of a soul shattering experience turning his life inside-out.

Some believe he immediately went to Jerusalem and then returned again to Tarsus. Others indicate he retired to Arabia for a prolonged period before asking Barnabas to present him to the other apostles in Jerusalem some time about 39 AD.

While the early part of his converted life is somewhat obscure, God has provided what we actually need to know. For example, when writing to the Galatians, Paul boldly announced he had not received his teaching from men (Galatians1:15-17). The reference seems to allude to Paul's unique training received from Christ while he was in Arabia.

After his escape from Damascus, it appears he fled into Arabia (Galatians 1:17). Some have speculated that he went to Sinai where, like Moses, he received his instruction from the Lord Jesus. However, there is absolutely no evidence for any specific location in Arabia. Sinai is surely possible, but we cannot be dogmatic about anything. We must adhere to only what the Scriptures authorize. What we do know is the Holy Spirit led him to whatever place or places he received the Word from the Lord.

It was in Arabia that the Lord Jesus interacted with Paul and taught him for an extended period of about three years. Was Paul caught up to heaven? Did Christ instruct him through visions? The details regarding this supernatural experience with Jesus are unknown. What we do know is he came from the experience with knowledge of things that Christ had not specifically taught the other apostles. The insight received would be the basis of his teaching about a new entity we know as *the Church.* From Jesus, he learned all he was to teach about the Church and her relationship to God and other vital details to be shared with others.

It becomes clear from the Scripture, Paul did not receive his commission nor his spiritual training from an earthly source. Why? Because, before he had any lengthy sessions with his former enemies (the apostles) he was taught by Christ alone. It also becomes apparent that Jesus had shared with Paul many things He had not taught His original disciples.

One may well ask: Why didn't Jesus teach all of the apostles the same doctrines? Biblical evidence indicates God has chosen to reveal His Truth *progressively.* Truth is revealed for the purpose of glorifying God and informing His people of His desire and what He wants them to know as His purposes unfold. Through *progressive revelation,* God tells us: (1) how to worship Him, (2) how we are related to Him, (3) what He is doing for us, (4) how we are to behave as His people, and (5) how we are to respond to the world through which we are passing.

The answer to why becomes clearer when you stop to consider that Jesus taught the first twelve apostles during a phase of His ministry when He emphasized being the Messiah and Israel's anticipated King. The disciples came from various walks of life, but they had one thing in common; they all had an expectation of a Messiah who would likely be a man analogous to Moses. A man who would lead them as a nation to overthrow the political and national powers oppressing them. Such was the theological and nationalistic climate into which the Lord Jesus was born, developed His ministry, and presented Himself as the sacrificial *Lamb of God.*[9]

The first disciples never expected Jesus to die a criminal's death as a substitute for man's sinfulness. The Messiah's death would have been a foreign concept to them. In the beginning, they likely thought Him to be a prophet with a special relationship with God like Moses. As time passed, it dawned on them Jesus was actually the Son of God (Matthew 16:16). These apostles who had attended Jesus' earthly ministry would not have a cognizant understanding of God's purpose through Christ until after His resurrection. Even then, they were floundering—wondering what to do and where to go. It was not until Jesus' ascent into heaven that the Holy Spirit had begun to progressively apply the Truth Jesus had taught them when they had experienced His physical presence.

It was nothing less than a miracle that on the day of Pentecost, God gave Peter an utterance by the Holy Spirit—he preached a summary of Israel's history showing them to be guilty of denying God

---

[9] In Part II of our book, we explain the *Mysteries of God* Jesus revealed to Paul in Arabia.

and rejecting Jesus as the promised Messiah who is truly the Son of God.

It was not until after Jesus' appearance to the disciples in their cloistered assembly that the Holy Spirit expanded Peter's understanding of the significance of Israel's sin in rejecting the Messiah. Peter, through his rooftop vision and Paul's witness, would soon understand. Setting Israel aside for a season, God began His focus on the salvation of Gentiles.

The Transition from Arabia to Jerusalem

Paul makes his first post conversion visit to Jerusalem (Acts 9:26-29). It is unclear why he had visited. It appears he might have done so at the encouragement of Barnabas who desired to have him meet the leaders of the believers. Judaism's leaders had officially charged him with heresy and many had set out to kill him. Conflicting reports swirled through Jerusalem. Even the believers were suspicious that Paul was a Jewish spy sent to identify leaders of the Jesus sect.

Under these conditions, Paul leaves Jerusalem and returns to Tarsus. His route took him by Caesarea (Acts 9:29,30). Soon after his arrival he accompanied Barnabas to visit Syria and Cilicia (Galatians 1:21-24).

Barnabas hastened to Tarsus to find Paul, because he wanted him to see what God was doing in the assemblies where Christ was preached. Paul accompanies Barnabas to Antioch (Acts 11:25-26). Paul observed first hand how many had responded to the witness of the believing Jews who had fled the persecution. He had limited his preaching to the Jews until they arrived in Antioch.

It was in Antioch that Gentiles were affected in growing numbers with their message. The Gentiles in Antioch, who had likely attended the synagogues, intently listening to know about the *new message*. Many were saved when they heard about Jesus being the Son of God. God's Word was working with miraculous saving power (Romans 1:16).

At some point during their Spiritually exhilarating visit, Agabus, a local prophet, predicted famine (Acts 11:27-29). The Holy Spirit impressed the assemblies to gather offerings for those being persecuted in Jerusalem. They asked Paul and Barnabas to carry the famine relief offering to Judea.

After they had completed their mission, Paul and Barnabas encouraged the brethren with reports about what God was doing abroad. They departed Jerusalem accompanied by John Mark (Acts 11:30; 12:25). They purposed to extend the preaching to other cities. This expedition would become known as the *First Missionary Journey.*

Questions for Discussion

1. Describe Paul's conversion experience.

2. Who did Saul receive his commission from as Paul an apostle?

3. Did Paul learn his doctrine from the other apostles? Explain your answer.

4. Who did Paul receive his training from as an Apostle and how long did it take initially?

5. Explain the concept of Progressive Revelation.

Chapter 3

First Missionary Journey

AD 48-49 (Acts 13:1-14:25)

Paul and Barnabas returned from delivering famine relief from the churches to the saints in Jerusalem and Judea. Some undisclosed time passes, and the Holy Spirit moved upon the leaders of the church at Antioch to appoint Barnabas and Paul to the work unto which He had called them (Acts 13:2). Having fasted, the assembly of believers commissioned Paul and Barnabas by laying hands on them.[10]

The Isle of Cypress (Acts 13:1-13)

The Holy Spirit led them to Seleucia on the Mediterranean Sea. They secured passage on a boat bound for Cyprus and landed at a port called Salamis. They made their way across the Island to Paphos where they encountered Elymas a sorcerer who was a false prophet. He was in the company of an official of the local government who desired to hear about God from Paul and Barnabas.

Paul immediately sensed evil when in the presence of Elymas. Therefore, he rebuked Elymas and pronounced a curse of blindness upon him. Paul did this because Elymas had hindered the preaching of God's Word. As a result of this stern rebuke, the un-named official obeyed the Lord's message to repent and believe on Christ. The Holy Spirit convicted him though Paul's preaching about Christ and the demonstration of the Lord's power by blinding the sorcerer (Acts 13:6-13).

Antioch of Pisidia (Acts 13:14-41)

When Paul and his party left Paphos in Pamphlia, John Mark left the mission and returned to Jerusalem. We do not know why John left, but Paul clearly did not like it. John Mark's behavior became a contentious affair briefly dividing Barnabas and Paul. (The sudden departure of John Mark illustrates how even in the early churches there were moments when an individual's desires

---

[10] The act of laying on hands symbolized official recognition by the Church. Those receiving the act were commissioned to carry out a particular service. In the case above Paul and Barnabas were approved for missionary work.

often divided brothers just as we experience in our day.)

The party departed from Perga and made the journey up from the Mediterranean to Antioch of Pisidia. They made arrangements for lodging and on the Sabbath day they attended the synagogue for worship. At the conclusion of the service Paul and his group were asked whether they had a word of encouragement for the congregation. (It might have been a polite gesture commonly afforded visitors from other synagogues.) Paul responded by standing and proceeded to outline the history of Israel from Moses, the judges, Samuel, Saul, and David. He then preached to them that Jesus was the Messiah from the linage of David. He showed them from the Psalms that Jesus is the promised one.

The message in the synagogue concluded with Paul declaring how faith in Jesus brings forgiveness of sins and justification before God, a justification that could not be granted through the law of Moses (Acts 13:38, 39).

There was much interest among some Jews and the Gentiles who had been present. The Gentiles were proselytes who regularly attended worship at the synagogue. They pressed Paul to speak again. The next Sabbath virtually the whole town had gathered to hear the Word of God. The Jews were jealous and began to rail against Paul and his party accusing them of blasphemy.

Anytime Truth is declared, it is a judgment against error. The guilty respond by attacking the messenger of Truth and accusing God's Truth as a bigoted idea. They consider the Truth unreasonable because they think it inhibits people in their attempt to live according to their own freewill. In the case of the Jews at Antioch, they refused to believe Jesus was the promised one. In rejecting Jesus they rejected the only one who could save them from sin. In their delusion, they assumed they were guaranteed salvation by obeying the Law as given by Moses. They thought turning to Jesus was to turn away from Moses. But in turning to Jesus (who kept the Law perfectly) they would actually affirm the Law as righteous.

Having been rejected by the Jews, Paul shifts his focus to the Gentiles. He will continue to preach to the Jews, but he now recognizes that his primary emphasis must be placed on those who will hear him. He probably remembered the witness of Ananias when the Lord Jesus told him Paul would be . . . *a chosen vessel unto me, to bear my name before the Gentiles, and kings, and the children of Israel (Acts 9:15).*

The Gentiles were hearing and receiving God's Word in large numbers wherever he went. Their hearts were not only curious; they were responsive to the message of salvation by grace through faith.

Iconium (Acts 14:1-5)

The mission party arrived in Iconium and went to the synagogue where they addressed both Jews and Greeks. Many believed and were received into the fellowship of the assembly. The unbelieving Jews, driven by their jealousy, stirred up the Gentiles causing them to resist the witness of Paul and his mission party (Acts 14:1-5).

After some time had been given to bold preaching about the grace of the Lord, signs and wonders were performed causing many to believe. We are not told what signs the Lord gave them, but those who witnessed could not legitimately deny that God was at work with these Jews from Jerusalem who were preaching Christ as the Messiah. However, there was a deep rift in the city's populace. Those against them planned to have them stoned, but God revealed the plot to the mission party, and they fled the city and came to Derbe and Lystra.

Region of Lycaonia (Acts 14:6-25)

Lycaonia is in a region located in central Asia called Galatia. It is a typical Greek city with its many gods and goddesses. Idolatry abounded. It was the principle region of the Spartan state. It came under the Roman Empire from around early second century BC until 395 AD.

Paul preached his Gospel in both Lystra and Derbe. These towns were in south central Asia. You will find Lystra about twenty miles south of Iconium. Located approximately another thirty miles southeast is Derbe. Little is known of these towns except Lystra was the home town of Timothy who became one of Paul's most faithful disciples. Timothy's mother Eunice and his grandmother Lois were faithful servants of the Lord (2 Timothy 1:5).

As was his custom, Paul addressed the synagogue gatherings before turning his focus toward the Gentiles. After hearing Paul's appeals, many came to faith in Christ.

In Lystra, Paul saw a man who had been lame and without the use of his feet for his entire life. As he was preaching, Paul noticed the man and his need. He perceived the crippled man believed his message. Therefore, in a loud voice Paul invited the man to stand to his feet. In the presence of the crowd, the man responded by being obedient, he leaped up and walked. The obvious miracle of God's healing the man gave credence to Paul's witness and many began to follow Christ.

The locals began to praise Barnabas and Paul. Some began to assign them names of deities. They called Barnabas, *Jupiter,* and Paul, *Mercury.* The priest of Jupiter brought oxen and garlands and were ready to offer sacrifice in their honor. Such behavior horrified Paul, and he objected declaring themselves mere men and not gods.

Paul appealed to them! He called out urging them to turn from false gods to the one true God, whose name is Jehovah, the Father of Jesus. God is the one who made all that exists including heaven and earth. He has given us abundance from the earth and gives rain from the heavens to quench our thirst and to bring an abundant harvest from the ground. Thus, Paul restrained the people from making sacrifice to them.

Somehow, Jews from Antioch and Iconium gained the attention of the people and stirred them up against Paul. The people became an unruly mob and the Jews led in stoning him. After the stoning, they dragged him out of the city thinking he was dead. Paul regained his consciousness and went into the city, and the next day departed for Derbe.

On the last leg of their first mission journey, Paul and his helpers returned again to Lystra, Iconium, and Antioch. They established or encouraged believers and appointed pastors to carry on the work of preaching and caring for the new believers. After praying, fasting, and committing them to the Gospel of grace, they encouraged them to continue in the faith. He warned them that much tribulation was coming.

Questions for Discussion

1. What ceremony did the church use to commission Paul and his mission team?

2. How did Paul deal with the magician he encountered on the Isle of Cypress?

3. What did John Mark do to cause conflict between Paul and Barnabas?

4. What did the Jews do to cause Paul to begin to focus on Gentile evangelism?

5. What was Paul's attitude when the local citizens in Lystria began to worship him?

Chapter 4

The Jerusalem Conference

AD 49 (Acts 14:26-28;15:1-39)

Having finished his first mission tour, he returned to Antioch, where they had first been commissioned by the assembly of believers now known as the Church at Antioch. Paul and Barnabas gathered the church and excitedly told them how God had opened the hearts of the Gentiles. He and Barnabas related the stories of God's work of salvation and how He had opened numerous opportunities to preach and minister in God's grace. They remained in Antioch for an extended time of rest (Acts 14:26-28).

Certain men came down from Judea teaching that Gentile believers had to be circumcised and had to keep the Law of Moses to be saved (Acts 15:1). Paul and Barnabas argued against the errors of these Jewish believers. There was considerable contention over the issues. The church decided to send representatives (including Paul and Barnabas) to the leaders of the Church at Jerusalem. Why? Because most believers considered Jerusalem as the center of authority for the witness of God's *Truth*. The representatives were to confer with the elders and apostles. The matter was urgent and needed clarification.

The entourage passed through Phoenicia and Samaria on their way to Jerusalem. As they traveled they shared what God was doing among the Gentiles and all believers rejoiced.

Arriving in Jerusalem, the committee likely experienced customary Jewish greetings and refreshment. After the church gathering was complete, the body included the elders, apostles, and all believers. The pastor, James, likely introduced the reason for their assembly and called for a report from the Church at Antioch. Paul and Barnabas made their report about the response of the Gentiles to the Gospel. He also shared about what God was doing through their witness. The church rejoiced! However, there arose a certain sect of believing Pharisees that said it was needful for the Gentiles to be circumcised and to keep the Law of Moses to be accepted by God (Acts 15:2-5).

The apostles and elders along with Barnabas and Paul entered into private counsel about the matter. After much disputing Peter rose up and said:

Acts 15:7-11

7 Men and brethren, ye know how that a good while ago God made choice among us, that the Gentiles by my mouth should hear the word of the gospel, and believe.
8 And God, which knoweth the hearts, bare them witness, giving them the Holy Ghost, even as he did unto us;
9 And put no difference between us and them, purifying their hearts by faith.
10 Now therefore why tempt ye God, to put a yoke upon the neck of the disciples, which neither our fathers nor we were able to bear?
11 But we believe that through the grace of the Lord Jesus Christ we shall be saved, even as they.

After Peter shared about how God made him aware he was to present the Gospel message to the Gentiles, the group then attentively listened to Paul and Barnabas' report on the miracles and acts of salvation God had wrought on their recent journey (Acts 15:12). Some Jewish believers who were Pharisees continued to object that even Gentile believers had to be circumcised and keep the Law. Paul had stood against the restrictive thinking of Judaizers in Antioch.

Even Peter and Barnabas had oscillated in their thinking at Antioch and had to be rebuked by Paul. The issue was critical for an effective Christian witness among the Gentiles; it had to be resolved once-and-for-all. Thus, the heated debate in Jerusalem became a doctrinal conflict between: (1) those who honored God's revelation about how He extended His focus of *grace* to the Gentiles (Acts 15:7), and (2) those who insisted that all believers must be circumcised and follow the Laws given through Moses. Paul's ultimate goal was to treat all believers with equal respect within the confines of their cultural background.

James, the pastor at Jerusalem, and convener of the conference, stood and made a formal proposal. The Holy Spirit records the conference conclusion in the passage below:

Acts 15:13-29

13 And after they had held their peace, James answered, saying, Men and brethren, hearken unto me:

14 Simeon hath declared how God at the first did visit the Gentiles, to take out of them a people for his name. 15 And to this agree the words of the prophets; as it is written,

16 After this I will return, and will build again the tabernacle of David, which is fallen down; and I will build again the ruins thereof, and I will set it up:

17 That the residue of men might seek after the Lord, and all the Gentiles, upon whom my name is called, saith the Lord, who doeth all these things.

18 Known unto God are all his works from the beginning of the world.

19 Wherefore my sentence is, that we trouble not them, which from among the Gentiles are turned to God:

20 But that we write unto them, that they abstain from pollutions of idols, and from fornication, and from things strangled, and from blood.

21 For Moses of old time hath in every city them that preach him, being read in the synagogues every sabbath day.

22 Then pleased it the apostles and elders, with the whole church, to send chosen men of their own company to Antioch with Paul and Barnabas; namely, Judas surnamed Barsabas, and Silas, chief men among the brethren:

23 And they wrote letters by them after this manner; The apostles and elders and brethren send greeting unto the brethren which are of the Gentiles in Antioch and Syria and Cilicia:

24 Forasmuch as we have heard, that certain which went out from us have troubled you with words, subverting your souls, saying, Ye must be circumcised, and keep the law: to whom we gave no such commandment:

25 It seemed good unto us, being assembled with one accord, to send chosen men unto you with our beloved Barnabas and Paul,

26 Men that have hazarded their lives for the name of our Lord Jesus Christ.

27 We have sent therefore Judas and Silas, who shall also tell you the same things by mouth.

28 For it seemed good to the Holy Ghost, and to us, to lay upon you no greater burden than these necessary things;

29 That ye abstain from meats offered to idols, and from blood, and from things strangled, and from fornication: from which if ye keep yourselves, ye shall do well. Fare ye well.

From the above passage, we discern certain vital information regarding behavior that will bring harmony between Jewish and Gentile believers.

The Jewish believers in Jerusalem agreed to accept Gentile believers on three conditions: (1) they abstain from identifying themselves with idols (29a), (2) they abstain from sexual immorality (:29b), and (3) they abstain from blood (29c).

One commentary states it this way:

> *All three prohibitions in Acts 15:20 are best taken in an ethical or moral sense. If this be so, they are still the responsibility of Christians today, even to the point of not eating blood sausage and raw meat. By not attending temple banquets, or being involved in fornication, or eating meat with blood in it, the Gentile Christians would be maintaining high moral standards and would keep from offending their Jewish brothers. There were Jews in every city who would be offended by Christians not following these strictures. These Israelites were well acquainted with these moral issues.*[11]

In this new understanding of faith in God, Jewish and Gentile believers are spiritually equal. The mandate from the Jerusalem conference ushered in a new era that some call the *age of grace*. The book of Acts is the story of the shift in our Father's focus from Israel to a new entity called the Church. As we will show in another chapter, God has spiritually blinded Israel as a nation for a season. There are prophecies that indicate that Israel will once again have a prominent place in God's purpose (Isaiah 61:5-6; Hosea 2:19; Zephaniah 3:20). (Abstaining from blood may be a reference to any of the following: eating strangled animals, eating raw meat, and some believe it to mean taking human life. Taking life was seen as shedding a person's blood because life is in the blood--Leviticus 17:11; I Samuel 17:5).

---

[11] Stanley D. Toussaint, *The Bible Knowledge Commentary: An Exposition of the Scriptures*, 1985, 2, 395–396.

Questions for Discussion

1. What action precipitated the official meeting in Jerusalem of the apostles and Church leaders?

2. Which apostle supported Paul by sharing his vision concerning the salvation of the Roman centurion?

3. Identify the two positions presented at the Jerusalem Council.

4. Who was the pastor at Jerusalem and what did he recommend to resolve the conflict?

5. According to the resolution in Jerusalem, both Jewish and Gentile believers in Jesus Christ are spiritually equal before God based on faith alone. (True or False) Why did you give your answer?

Chapter 5

Second
Missionary Journey

AD 49-51 (Acts 15:36-18:22)

After some extended time, Judas, the prophet or preacher, returned to Jerusalem with greetings from the church at Antioch along with their concurrence with the findings of *the Jerusalem council* (Acts 15:33). Paul, Barnabas and Silas remained to minister the Word among the believers of Antioch. (Acts 15:35).

Impressed of the Lord, Paul decided to return to the churches that the Lord had previously led him to establish. He desired to determine their spiritual state. Barnabas desired to take John Mark as an assistant in ministry. However, Paul was opposed to the idea because John Mark had abandoned them earlier in Pamphylia. The disagreement became so divisive that Barnabas chose John Mark and sailed for Cyprus, and Paul made other plans (Acts 15:37-39). Being commended by the church at Antioch, Paul chose Silas and traveled through Syria and Cilicia where they began to spiritually strengthen the churches with the Truth Jesus had taught him. (Acts 15:40, 41).

Spiritual encouragement can only come through ingested Truth. Truth bolsters faith in God and promotes obedience out of love and not fear.

Derbe and Lystra (Acts 16:1-5)

When Paul reached Derbe and Lystra, God had arranged an appointment for Paul to meet a young man named Timothy who had a Jewish mother and a Gentile father. He had become a believer and had been well reported of by other Christians in Lystra and Iconium. Paul invited Timothy to join his missionary party. Paul was bearing a testimony to both Jew and Gentile; therefore, because he was coming under the scrutiny of the Jews, he needed to circumcise Timothy. Paul performed this rite on Timothy so that he would not be offensive to the Jews when he witnessed to them about Jesus being the Christ.

As the missionary team went through the various cities, they preached Christ and informed the people of the three things that they must do to avoid being offensive to the Jewish believers.

Many believers from Jewish and Gentile backgrounds wrestled with how to harmonize their differences with their new faith in the Lord Jesus. Their commitment to the Commandments of God caused the Jewish believers to expect believing Gentiles to keep at least four spiritual precepts from the Law that had been agreed on at the Jerusalem council (Acts15:29).

This was the beginning of Timothy's training to become an evangelist and pastor for Christ. Paul proceeded to mentor Timothy. His experience with Paul would prepare him to invest himself in the lives of others. Following Paul's example, Timothy would invest himself in faithful men. In turn those faithful men would do the same for others (2 Timothy 2:2).

They continued their work through out Phrygia and the region of Galatia. The mission team was successful in building up the churches through Christian doctrine. The Holy Spirit led Paul to appoint qualified men as leaders for continued spiritual development of the various congregations. The spiritual soundness of the churches resulted in a daily increase in their numbers (Acts 16:5).

Paul believed in planning. The fact he planned is evident by Luke informing his readers of Paul's desire to go into Asia with Christ's message. However, he also tells us the Holy Spirit hindered Paul's plan and directed him to Troas.

Luke's account of Paul's plans for preaching in Asia should teach us that planning is a necessary activity, but not at the expense of following the Holy Spirit. God has the right to alter our steps but that does not mean we should not plan. It simply means we must always submit our plans to the Father for His approval.

Troas (Acts 16:6-10)

As they had passed by Mysia, they desired to go to Bithynia, but the Spirit refused to give them permission. Luke's record encourages us because we know that the Holy Spirit directs us today just as He directed Paul on his mission journeys. He does so in much the same manner as He did with Paul (John 14:17, 26).

We must never forget that God is our champion and continues to lead and enable His people in the missions whereto He has called them. The Holy Spirit has final authority with the right to re-direct our plans. He may deny us certain opportunities while providing us with new ones. He is always right, He will never lead us into error, and will protect us as we obey Him.

While in Troas, Paul had a vision of a Macedonian bidding him to come and help him (Acts 16:8). Paul responded immediately by setting a direct course to Philppi. His travel plans took him on a route by-passing Samothracia and Neapolis.

Philippi (Acts 16:18-40)

Philippi was a major population center named after Philip II, King of Macedonia and father of Alexander the Great. It was populated by Roman colonists, native Greeks, and Orientals. There were many Jews among the Greeks and Orientals. It was the westernmost district of Europe and is presently identified as part of Greece. The Gospel penetrated Europe under the Holy Spirit's direction. Paul's second missionary journey was the beginning of Christian expansion that would ultimately engulf

Europe and the Americas. Western civilization would become the launching pad for world-wide Christian mission activity for centuries to come.

The mission team visited a worship and prayer service by the river on their first Sabbath day in Philippi. The team joined some who had gathered for prayer. While there, they met a woman named Lydia from Thyatira who worshiped God. Lydia was a business woman who was probably in Philippi to sell her fabrics. As she had listened to Paul talk about the Lord Jesus, the Lord opened her heart and she believed.

After she and her family were baptized, she invited Paul and those with him to her home to abide there while they ministered the Word in Philippi (Acts 16:15). According to the Bible record Lydia was the first woman in the region to receive Christ. Her salvation might have been a gateway to Christianity's influence on Western civilization. The ministry in Philippi was an undetermined extended stay.

On one occasion, when they were on their way to the place designated for prayer (near the river), a demon possessed girl followed them and shouted as she followed . . . *These are the servants of the most high God, which shew unto us the way of salvation (Acts 16:17).* A spirit of divination possessed the girl. It was a spirit that enabled her to supernaturally know some things about the future. The Greek scholar Marvin Vincent provides us with historical and cultural insight into the passage by sharing with us what the people of Philippi would likely have thought about the possessing spirit.

> *The heathen inhabitants of Philippi regarded the woman as inspired by Apollo; and Luke, in recording this case, which came under his*

own observation, uses the term which would naturally suggest itself to a Greek physician, a Python-spirit, presenting phenomena identical with the convulsive movements and wild cries of the Pythian priestess at Delphi.[12]

Luke identifies the girl as demon possessed because the Holy Spirit revealed to him the possessing spirit was Satan's underling. The girl was being used as a medium by the spirit. Others used her supernatural powers for financial gain. This continued for many days. At some point Paul became irritated by her following them. He turned and with apostolic authority said . . . *I command thee in the name of Jesus Christ to come out of her (Acts 16:18).* God's Spirit freed her in that very hour. She was no longer under the dominating influence of the possessing spirit. [13]

The maiden's handlers were no longer able to use the girl for financial gain, because the demon of divination could not provide her with supernatural insight. Why? Because it had been cast out of her. Therefore, because of their loss of income, these mystic entrepreneurs became angry and incited the citizens against Paul and Silas and forcibly brought them before the magistrates. They were charged with disturbing the customs of the city, and teaching things they thought called into question the supremacy of Rome. The city officials had them beaten and turned them over to the jailor who placed their feet in stocks and put them in the most secure part of the prison.

---

[12] Marvin Richardson Vincent, *Word Studies in the New Testament*, (New York: Charles Scribner's Sons, 1887), 1:531.

[13] For an explanation of demonic activity see our book *Our Unseen Enemy.*

Scripture records that at midnight, in the inner prison, Paul and Silas were singing praises to God. Suddenly, there was an earthquake of such magnitude the prison doors were opened and the prisoners shackles fell off. The jailor, fearing the prisoners had escaped, drew his sword to kill himself. Paul called out to him . . . *Do thyself no harm: for we are all here (Acts 16:28).* The jailor immediately called for a light and came with great anxiety to Paul and Silas and asked . . . *What must I do to be saved? And they said, Believe on the Lord Jesus Christ, and thou shalt be saved, and thy house (Acts 16:30).*

The jailor secured the prisoners and had Paul and Silas brought into his living quarters where they were fed and their wounds cared for. The family listened intently as Paul and Silas shared the message about Jesus. The jailor and all his family believed and followed the Lord in baptism. The faithfulness of Paul and Silas bore fruit on that fateful night with the salvation of a whole family.

The number of believers was growing in Philippi. Soon, probably the next day, a directive arrived from the magistrate to release Paul and Silas. The magistrates likely realized they had erred in arresting them and desired to settle the matter privately.

Paul, being a Roman citizen, refused to leave prison until the magistrates exonerated them. The prisoners had been arrested publicly and Paul reasoned and insisted they be released publicly which he likely thought would exonerate them in the eyes of the citizens. When the city officials realized Paul was a Roman and they had illegally beaten them without a trial, they came and publicly released them from prison asking that they leave the city.

Leaving jail Paul and Silas went to the home of Lydia and ministered to her and other believers. The apostle and his fellow laborers comforted them before continuing their journey.

Thessalonica (Acts 17:5-9)

Leaving Philippi, the mission party including Paul, Silas, and likely Luke, passed through Amphipolis and Apollonia. They came to Thessalonica where there was a Jewish synagogue.

Thessalonica was a major population center and gateway to the heart of Europe. This might have been one of the reasons that the Holy Spirit directed him there. At the northern end of the Aegean Sea, Thessalonica was a major trade center; it was home to a diverse population including many Jews who had established a synagogue for worship and learning. Paul spent several sabbaths there preaching and reasoning from the Old Testament Scriptures about Jesus being the Messiah and why He was crucified, buried, resurrected, and then ascended into heaven. Some of the Jews believed Paul's reasoned message and desired to follow Jesus as the Christ. God had opened their spiritual eyes by drawing them to Christ. A great multitude of the devout Gentiles present also believed (Acts 17:1-4).

The Good News about Jesus being the Christ aggravated unbelieving Jews, and they conspired against Paul and those with him. They even bribed some unprincipled cronies to bring trumped up charges against Paul and his associates. It appears the Jews formed a posse and went to the home of

Jason where it was reported Paul and his mission team had lodged. When the angry mob of unbelieving Jews arrived at Jason's home, they did not find Paul. Therefore, they dragged Jason and likely those present before the authorities and accused them of conspiring with Paul causing sedition, thereby opposing Roman authority. After posting bail, Jason and his friends were released.

The believers implored Paul to leave Thessalonica because of the Jewish inspired rebellion against his message. After counseling him about the matter, they quietly ushered Paul and Silas under the darkness of night out of the city. The believers continued to grow in grace. Their numbers increased under the harsh intolerance of Jewish persecution.

Berea (Acts 17:10-15)

Loyal supporters ushered Paul and Silas out of town to avoid subjecting them to the harassment of angry unbelieving Jews. They traveled west and came to Berea, as was their manner upon entering a city, they sought out the Jewish Synagogue. Paul always presented the Gospel to the Jews first before turning to the Gentiles. Members of the synagogue were likely a mixture of Pharisees and Sadducees.

He clearly proved himself a loyal adherent to the teachings of Moses. Paul did not reject the teaching of Moses: what he rejected was the refusal of the Jewish leaders to receive Jesus as the Messiah. He remained a practicing Jew because he did not wish to offend his fellow Jews. However, as with Christ, the Jewish religion rejected Paul and pushed him and all believing Jews out of the Jewish fold.

As Paul preached about Jesus, many of them listened intently as he shared from the Scriptures how Jesus was the fulfillment of the Law and that He is the long anticipated Messiah. Many of his hearers believed and desired to know more. Among them were many *noble* Gentile men and some believing women who were people of influence in Berea.

The believers at Berea were unique. The characteristic that set them apart from others was they insisted on testing what was being taught. The Bible informs us they searched the Scriptures daily to affirm the preaching of Paul and Silas was true. Bible teachers for centuries have cited the Berean believers for dependence on the Scriptures as the authoritative Word of God. They were driven by a higher commitment to what they knew came from God. They had a reputation for comparing all teaching with what the Lord says in His Word.

The church in this current century would do well to follow the Berean example. If believers do not adopt an attitude of dependence upon what God teaches in His Word, we are doomed to the error of human opinion and philosophy. It appears that in our generation people feel their opinion is all that matters.

It is a huge eternal risk to reject the clear testimony of God in favor of your own human reasoning. The Lord has warned man, *Trust in the Lord with all your heart; and lean not unto thine own understanding* (Proverbs 3:5). To ignore the above principle is to place yourself in spiritual jeopardy and possibly eternal death. Never forget there are consequences when disregarding the plain instruction of God. [14]

Upon hearing of Paul's success in Berea, the discontented Jews in Thessalonica took it upon themselves to bring their disruption to Paul's Berean mission. It appears the Jews hatred was primarily focused on Paul. These seditious seducers immediately stirred up the public against Paul causing an uproar in the city. The turmoil was so great that some of the believers counseled Paul to leave. Silas and Timothy remained. Why? It may have been to help the new believers to understand better their relationship to Christ.

The Scripture records some Berean believers quietly accompanied Paul as he followed their counsel and departed for Athens. Luke does not tell us anything about where Paul settles in Athens. The city was huge by 33 AD standards. It was perhaps the world's largest cultural and intellectual center. The glory of Greece had past, for it was no longer a world power but was now in subjugation to Rome. However, it was still renowned as the gathering place of deeply serious thinkers and philosophers. Athens was thought to have had more gods than people.

We are not told anything about his initial ministry there. In all likelihood, he sought out a synagogue in which to observe corporate worship because he had not yet abandoned Judaism.

---

[14] In the twenty-first century, people commonly take the position that if they think something to be true, then their perception makes it true. For example, many today feel Hell is not real, others believe there is no God, and some actually believe that if there is a Heaven all will go there. According to the Bible, none of the aforementioned are true. **Truth is what God says, not what man thinks.**

His friends from Berea prepared themselves to return home. Paul asked them to inform Silas and Timothy to join him in Athens.

Athens (Acts 17:16-34)

In Athens, Paul's spirit is stirred within him as he observes the open idolatry of the people. He had encountered idolatry before, but never on this scale. He likely spent some time before the Lord as he waited for his co-workers to arrive from Berea. He must have sought the Holy Spirit's wisdom about what strategy he should use to introduce the Gospel to this huge metropolis.

On the sabbath day Paul met with the Jews and devout seekers at the synagogue. However, during the week he went into the market place engaging whoever would give him a hearing. He did not use the same approach as he had with the Jews. Why? Because, these pagans had no knowledge of Israel's history nor were they aware of the true God Jehovah. Remember, with the Jews he argued from Scripture that Christ was the Messiah. Here, he seeks a common ground with the people from which to launch his message about God's saving grace. It appears he departed from his usual approach to his preaching ministry.

As previously, he began in the local synagogue, but then his ministry focus changed. He turned his attention to the very center of human intellectual sophistication and philosophy. The religions of Greece were pagan in nature, but were based on eminently developed world-views governed by pagan thinking. Their religious systems of thought even answered some of the basic questions that haunt mankind. Who are we? Where did we come from? Why are we here? What is our purpose? Paul would have to effectively show that revelation from Israel's true God is superior to man's preconceived imaginations about what gods should be or do.

He evidently began engaging people in the gathering places by discussing their thinking about life. While he was doubtlessly outraged by their idolatry, he had compassion on them because of their ignorance. Someone said: *there were more gods in Athens than there were people.* To those who would listen, he unfolded the message of the true God who sent His Son to die for the sins of the world. He would go on to show that God's Son Jesus has authority to forgive sin. Jesus proved who He was by His many miraculous acts and by raising some like Lazarus from the dead.

It was not long before the Epicureans and Stoics heard about Paul and his God. The Holman Commentary reminds us that the Epicureans and Stoics were only two of the many world-view systems existing at the time. And if we are talking about our current world, it says: *We could substitute pragmatism, utilitarianism, atheism, agnosticism, communism, or a host of other more modern philosophies.*[15] We must remember, all reasoning of sinful man competes with the Truth of God's revelation.

These philosophers urged Paul to come to Mars' Hill (the court of the Areopagites) where this *new* teaching could be heard by the court. They were particularly interested in Paul's account of Jesus' resurrection.

Do not confuse the occasion with a formal court hearing. It was more like a platform where

---

[15] Kenneth O. Gangel, Acts, Holman New Testament Commentary, (Nashville, TN: Broadman & Holman Publishers, 1998), 5:288.

ideas were presented to influential members of the intellectual society. There were no official judgments passed regarding societal governmental laws. They deliberated among themselves the values of the things they heard. These world influencing thinkers and philosophers were proud of their tolerance concerning opposing world-views and multitudes of religions. It was in this setting that Paul began his discourse about an altar in Athens marked to honor the *Unknown God*.

In the above context we have the following verse:

Acts 17:22

Then Paul stood in the midst of Mars' hill, and said, Ye men of Athens, I perceive that in all things ye are too superstitious.

Paul had accompanied his inquisitors to the very heart of their stronghold. It was here the Gospel would compete with the philosophies of men and demons.

He begins his address by acknowledging what they may have thought to be a word of praise when he said: I perceive that in all things ye are too superstitious. The phrase used in the King James version is correct, but too superstitious would be better understood in our vernacular as very religious.

The statement would not have been offensive to the people of Athens because they were proud of their many gods and arrogantly thought their various systems of belief were superior to all others. Thus, in this environment Paul begins his presentation of the Gospel.

He continues . . .

Acts 17:23

For as I passed by, and beheld your devotions, I found an altar with this inscription, TO THE UNKNOWN GOD. Whom therefore ye ignorantly worship, him declare I unto you.

His reference to their devotions is an acknowledgment they had many idols. [16] Instead of condemning them for idol worship, he draws their attention to the altar marked TO THE UNKNOWN GOD. He states his desire to introduce them to this God whom they ignorantly worship.[17] The charge they were ignorant is not meant to be an offensive slur, but, an observation of the fact they do not know this true God about whom he wishes to inform them.

Acts 17:24

God that made the world and all things therein, seeing that he is Lord of heaven and earth, dwelleth not in temples made with hands;

Paul says three things about the true God (1) He is the creator of all things, (2) He is sovereign, thereby controlling all His creation and (3) He does not dwell in temples made by His creatures because

---

[16] Based on Paul's first letter to the church at Corinth (1 Corinthians 10:20, 21), he made the point that when people worship idols they are in reality worshipping demons. However in Athens, he attempts to introduce the *Unknown God* as Jehovah who is the only true God. Therefore, Paul insists there is only one God!

[17] The reason the Greeks had an altar to the UNKNOWN GOD was to avoid offending any god that they might have failed to identify. In all probability, each Greek had several gods he worshiped. They perceived a god could only function or protect in one or two areas of life; therefore, each person needed several gods to meet various needs.

His presence is everywhere. Paul's statement is significant because:

> *The most profound philosophers of Greece were unable to conceive any real distinction between God and the universe. Thick darkness, therefore, behooved to rest on all their religious conceptions. To dissipate this, the apostle sets out with a sharp statement of the fact of creation as the central principle of all true religion—not less needed now, against the transcendental idealism of our day.*[18]

All false religions build their belief systems on faulty pre-conceived ideas about God. The only reason the Jews and Christians are the exception is because God has revealed Himself to them. All religions that do not begin their belief system based on God's revelation of Himself are false and doomed to propagate error.

> *Acts 17:25-26*
>
> *25 Neither is worshipped with men's hands, as though he needed any thing, seeing he giveth to all life, and breath, and all things; 26 And hath made of one blood all nations of men for to dwell on all the face of the earth, and hath determined the times before appointed, and the bounds of their habitation;*

Paul continues to share characteristics of the true God who is unknown to them. Note the following: (1) The true God is the source and sustainer of all life; therefore, He has no needs because He is complete in Himself; (2) God has

---

[18] Robert Jamieson, A. R. Fausset, and David Brown, *Commentary Critical and Explanatory on the Whole Bible*, (Oak Harbor, WA: Logos Research Systems, Inc., 1997), 2:202.

created man of one blood to dwell on this earth; therefore, all races are linked by their humanness and ultimately to a common ancestry in Adam and Eve; (3) in His sovereignty, God has determined the destiny of the nations and their boundaries. The third claim is difficult for fallen man to accept. Why? Because, we like to think ourselves to be in control of our own destiny. God made man in His likeness. However, man has a limited sovereignty whereas our Creator has unlimited sovereignty and that should explain the distinction.

Based upon Paul's declaration in verse twenty-six that God is sovereign over the nations and their boundaries, we know it is the Lord who causes nations and leaders to rise and fall. It is He who determines the various parameters of the world's nations.[19] Henceforth, believers should rest in the Lord knowing that all things work together for the good of those who are committed to God's purpose (Romans 8:28,29).

Philosophers in Athens were familiar with some of the concepts shared by Paul. However, contrary to Paul's instruction, they thought the Unknown God needed them and what their hands could offer and that they in turn could earn His favor through their worship. The concept of God's unlimited sovereignty would likely be problematic for them as it is for so many in all ages.

After informing them about the Unknown God, Paul begins to instruct them about how to approach God. Notice the next few verses.

Acts 17:27

---

[19] Many Christians will disagree with this statement. However, I appeal to you to take Paul's plain statement at face value and interpret it on that basis.

27 That they should seek the Lord, if haply
they might feel after him, and find him, though
he be not far from every one of us:

Paul paints a picture of man seeking after God as one feeling his way in the dark. Darkness is a state created by man himself. Paul reminds us in Romans . . . *there is none that seeketh after God . . .(Romans 3:11)* (As fallen men, sin darkens our minds. Therefore, in our present condition, we do not try to find God because doing so would bring us to His light and His light would expose our sins. Placing oneself in such a state is intolerable to one who denies the existence of his sin. Therefore, although He is near, God will not be found. God bestows life to all created beings, and He sustains them in their life environment until He choses to remove them from their earthly condition through physical death over which God alone is sovereign.) There is a hint of Pantheism in the verse and the ones to follow. However, Paul is not teaching the erroneous doctrine of Pantheism.[20]

28 For in him we live, and move, and have our
being; as certain also of your own poets have
said, For we are also his offspring.

Paul reminds his listeners: not only are we created by God, but He sustains our life. God creates and sustains us and in that sense, we are His offspring, and the loving focus of His creation. However, He has chosen to only show His ultimate love of salvation through grace and adoption to those who receive His only begotten Son Jesus.

---

[20] Pantheists believe God is in everything and God is everything. Pantheistic thinking is wrong because God is a separate entity from His creation. Just because He is everywhere, everywhere is not God.

29 Forasmuch then as we are the offspring of God, we ought not to think that the Godhead is like unto gold, or silver, or stone, graven by art and man's device.

Through God's act of creation man is seen as His offspring. Recognizing the true God as the creator of all things, we are not to liken Him to gold, silver, or anything we can fashion with our hands. To do so is to reduce the Godhead or Divine essence to graven art made by the hands of men. There is no temple or other created thing that can contain Him. He is present everywhere, He knows all things, and He has all power.

Paul reminds us that all idols like those in Athens are made by the promptings of demons that seek the worship of men (1 Corinthians 10:20).

30 And the times of this ignorance God winked at; but now commandeth all men every where to repent:

Through the centuries, God has winked at or tolerated man's ignorant worship of idols. Now, at this very moment, God commands men in all the earth to repent.

You may ask, repent of what?

All men must repent of their sin of not worshipping the true God. To show their repentance, they must recognize their sin, confess it, and appeal to God for mercy on the grounds of the resurrected Savior's sacrifice. The Lord Jesus has promised to forgive all who will, in faith, appeal to Him based on His substitutionary death for the sins of all men in all times (Romans 5:6).

31 Because he hath appointed a day, in the which he will judge the world in righteousness by that man whom he hath ordained; whereof he hath given assurance unto all men, in that he hath raised him from the dead.

God's demand for all men everywhere to repent is not a heartless or ruthless order. It is an urgent appeal offered in love for all to become compliant with what He has created us for. He urges us to repent because an appointed day of judgment is coming and all will be held accountable. The One who judges will be the One who died and rose again to give us victory over sin.

32 And when they heard of the resurrection of the dead, some mocked: and others said, We will hear thee again of this matter.
33 So Paul departed from among them.
34 Howbeit certain men clave unto him, and believed: among the which was Dionysius the Areopagite, and a woman named Damaris, and others with them.

Faithfully preaching the Bible will always produce a response. Some will hear in unbelief and will mock the preacher and the Truth; some will ponder it but not commit to it; and others will joyfully respond in faith and believe the Word. Jesus' parable of the sower illustrates this principle (Luke 8:4-14). Like Paul and others who believed through God's witness, we must in faith share the very Word we have received.

Corinth (Acts 18:1-22)

Leaving the Areopagus and Athens, Paul made his way to the coastal city of Corinth located forty miles west. By the standards of New Testament times, Corinth was a large trading metropolis. It was one of the major crossroads in that part of the

world and was intersected by severa'
lanes. The city was morally dece
idolatrous.

Upon arrival Paul soon came upon a Jewiṣɪ
tent-making couple named Aquila and Priscilla. The
couple came to Corinth because they had been
forced to leave Rome by edict of the emperor
Claudius. It appeared to be a divine appointment by
which Paul would develop a strong Jewish ally with
a common vocation. Why? Maybe it was because
Paul's father had taught him the tent-making trade.

It is unclear when Aquila and Priscilla became
Christians. Historians disagree; some believe they
were already believers when they arrived from
Rome, and some believe them to be converts from
Paul's preaching in the synagogue at Corinth.
However, this is certain, Paul dwelled with these
devout believers and worked with them maintaining
a strong witness to the Jewish community and to
the Gentiles who were interested in the true God.
Out of financial necessity, Paul used his skills as a
craftsman to earn his livelihood. He worked
alongside his hosts making tents and maybe
upholstering furniture.

When Paul came to Athens from Berea in
Macedonia, he left Silas and Timothy there to
strengthen the church. After some undisclosed
time, his comrades joined him in Corinth. Upon
their arrival he experienced a renewed boldness in
his preaching. He preached with more fervor the
message Jesus is the Christ. His ardor produced
the same result in Corinth as it had everywhere
else. *The Bible Knowledge Commentary* makes the
following observation concerning the arrival of Silas
and Timothy:

Timothy's arrival encouraged Paul: (1) The pair evidently brought financial aid from Macedonia (cf. 2 Cor. 11:9; Phil 4:15). Because of this monetary gift it was no longer necessary for Paul to pursue a trade and he could give himself totally to the work of the gospel. (2) The good news about the steadfastness of the Thessalonian church refreshed Paul (cf. 1 Thes. 3:6–8). (3) Their companionship would have been an encouragement to the apostle.[21]

Every Sabbath he shared in the synagogue persuading both Jew and Gentile. When the Jews continually resisted his witness, in a declaration of finality, he said . . .*Your blood be upon your own heads; I am clean: from henceforth, I will go unto the Gentiles (Acts 18:6).*

Although most Jews rejected Paul's witness, the Holy Spirit used him to gather together a sizable band of believers, composed of both Jews and Gentiles, to begin following the Savior. Now that fellow laborers had arrived with financial support from the churches in Macedonia, he could give more of his time to the ministry without being concerned about how he would make a living. There seems to have been an increase in ministry results when he left Aquila and Priscilla and took up residence with Titus Justus. He remained in Corinth about eighteen months.

Sometime after his renewed zeal, dissenting Jews brought charges against Paul before Gallio, an official of the province of Achaia. He was charged with blasphemy. The charges were dismissed

---

[21] Stanley D. Toussaint, *The Bible Knowledge Commentary: An Exposition of the Scriptures*, 1985, 2, 405.

because they were of a religious nature and not an offense against Rome.

Paul and his party remain in Antioch in Pisidia about a year. At the end of this time he takes a boat to Caesarea and from there he goes up to Jerusalem to complete his previous vow to God (Acts18:21, 22).

Jamison, Fausset, and Brown have a succinct word to share about these verses.

> *In these few words does the historian despatch the apostle's fourth visit to Jerusalem after his conversion. The expression "going up" is invariably used of a journey to the metropolis; and thence he naturally "went down to Antioch." Perhaps the vessel reached too late for the feast, as he seems to have done nothing in Jerusalem beyond "saluting the Church," and privately offering the sacrifice with which his vow (Ac 18:18) would conclude. It is left to be understood, as on his arrival from his first missionary tour, that "when he was come, and had gathered the church together, he rehearsed all that God had done with him" (Ac 14:27) on this his second missionary journey.*[22]

If our cited commentators are correct, Paul followed a similar pattern of greeting and sharing with the Jerusalem church after each mission enterprise. Leaving Jerusalem he returned to Antioch which had become the missionary headquarters of the church.

---

[22] Robert Jamieson, A. R. Fausset, and David Brown, *Commentary Critical and Explanatory on the Whole Bible*, (Oak Harbor, WA: Logos Research Systems, Inc., 1997), 2:204.

Questions for Discussion

1.   What caused Paul to initiate a second mission tour?

2.   What was wrong with the maiden who followed Paul in
      Philippi and what were the repercussions?

3.   What were the Bereans noted for?

4.   Why is it important to study Paul's message from Mars
      hill?

5.   What was Paul's response to the Jews in the Athenian
      synagogue who rejected his message about Jesus?

Chapter 6

Third
Missionary Journey

AD 54-58 (Acts 18:23-21:26)

Paul's understanding of Christ's teaching has matured and the secret things of God have begun to find expression through his teaching in both precept and action. We must not let our appreciation of Paul or any other apostle elevate to the station of worship. No man is to be worshipped except Christ (Who is God indwelling flesh - John 1:1). When we read the exploits of Paul and other apostles, it is easy to become enamored with an exaggerated sense of hero worship. We must resist!

Why? Because all men have failings and will disappoint us. The Scriptures attest to this principle repeatedly. For example, David, Moses, Solomon, and even the Lord's apostles had feet of *clay,* meaning they were flawed as are all *sin-natured* men.

I do not call this to your attention to discourage you or to provide you with an excuse for your own sins. I merely wish to remind you that in our present state, we continue to wrestle with the *old man or sin nature* (Romans 7). We need to profit from Paul's teachings while realizing we have not *arrived* just because we are Christians. God is not through with us yet! We are a work in progress as was Paul.[23]

Ephesus (Acts 18:24-19:41)

For now, we refocus on Paul's mission efforts as recorded below.

Acts 19:1-7

And it came to pass, that, while Apollos was at Corinth, Paul having passed through the upper coasts came to Ephesus: and finding certain disciples,
2 He said unto them, Have ye received the Holy Ghost since ye believed? And they said unto him, We have not so much as heard whether there be any Holy Ghost.
3 And he said unto them, Unto what then were ye baptized? And they said, Unto John's baptism.
4 Then said Paul, John verily baptized with the baptism of repentance, saying unto the

---

[23] In the section on mysteries, we will soon discover the enabling principles for living as victorious Christians.

people, that they should believe on him which
should come after him, that is, on Christ
Jesus.
5 When they heard this, they were baptized in
the name of the Lord Jesus.
6 And when Paul had laid his hands upon
them, the Holy Ghost came on them; and they
spake with tongues, and prophesied.
7 And all the men were about twelve.

In about 52 AD a young Jew named Apollos from Egypt's Alexandria came to Ephesus and preached eloquently in the synagogue. His spiritual discernment impressed Aquila and Priscilla. He had been taught the Old Testament Scriptures well. However he had not been introduced to Jesus. He was only familiar with the teachings of John and his baptism unto repentance. After hearing Apollos preach, Aquila and Priscilla purposed to take him under their care to tutor him in the faith. From the Scriptures they instructed him about Jesus being the Messiah. Being a quick study, he matured rapidly in his belief about Jesus being the Christ. Soon he was championing Christ and proving from the Scriptures Jesus was the Messiah. He regularly defended Christ in the synagogue. Luke wrote that Apollos left Ephesus for Antioch of Pisidia (Acts 19:1-7). He carried with him letters of commendation from the believers.

Meanwhile Paul leaves Antioch for Ephesus. Upon arrival, he becomes aware of about twelve disciples who had not received the Holy Spirit. Paul asked, unto whom were they baptized? They replied, John's baptism. After hearing Paul's Gospel message, they were baptized in the name of Jesus and received the Holy Spirit.

From the above record it seems that Paul makes a distinction between John's baptism unto repentance and the apostles baptism in Christ's name which we call the baptism of faith. The *baptism unto repentance* was the baptism John provided upon reception of his message to repent when he preached in Judea. The *baptism of faith* was the baptism the apostles provided to those receiving their message of personal faith in Christ. (It was given when one personally believed that Christ died for his sins.)

They preached Christ is the Messiah and Savior of all who believe on Him. John was preaching under the authority of the Old Covenant and the apostles were preaching under the authority of The New Covenant. One Truth Paul reveals is this: believers in Christ are baptized by the Holy Spirit into a spiritual reality known as *The Body of Christ*. These Ephesians had not received a spiritual baptism by the Holy Spirit. Therefore, as Christians are defined today, they were not yet Christians. The event provides us with yet another proof of a definitive transition from Judaism to Christianity.

It appears that the Holy Spirit did not have Luke record every ministry event or location for Paul and his emissaries. From the historian's perspective, we do not have all the dates and places wrapped in a tidy package. However, we rest confident in this: we have all we need for spiritual understanding.

The year is approximately 54 AD and Paul had tarried in Antioch of Syria until about 57 AD. From Ephesus he wrote his first letter to the church at Corinth containing four major points: (1) he instructed them in church polity, (2) he corrected them concerning schisms and doctrines, (3) he dealt with church discipline regarding a member who was immoral, and (4) he taught them about the ordinance of the Lord's Supper and spiritual gifts.

Leaving Ephesus, Paul traveled through Galatia, and Phrygia (Acts 18:23). He revisited the various churches to ensure they were strengthened in the faith. Timothy is sent to Corinth with Paul's urgent epistle in hand (1 Corinthians 4:17). Later, he returns to Ephesus to encourage them in face of his former rebuke (1 Corinthians 16:10-11).

Paul preached in the synagogue for three months until the discussions became so fractious that he needed to relocate for the sake of peace. Paul would not compromise his message about Jesus being the Messiah. The Jews contended his preaching was heretical and not in accordance with Jewish tradition. At some point, Tyrannus, a teacher of rhetoric, invited Paul to use his lecture hall for his discussions about the Messiah (Acts 19:8-10). We think Tyrannus was either a lecturer or philosopher who had come to believe on Christ and therefore had invited Paul to use his lecture hall for his teaching. Paul utilized Tyrannus' facility for two years. At some point, he sends Timothy and Erastus to proceed him into Macedonia (Acts 19:21). Later, when the Lord directed him, he too left Ephesus for Macedonia.

Troas (Acts 20:6-12)

On his way to Macedonia Paul stops at Troas hoping to meet with Titus (Acts 20:1; 2 Corinthians 2:13). These actions imply that he is effectively using his team to an optimum degree to accomplish his mission. We, in the twenty-first century, must ascertain from these biblical events the Holy Spirit utilized the personalities of men as well as their human intellect to accomplish God's purpose among men. He only uses His supernatural power in the affairs of men when it furthers His cause and predetermined will. God is not an egotistical showoff.

The citizenry in Ephesus observed many miracles. Using Paul as an instrument, God healed many sicknesses and others He freed from demonic bondage. These miraculous acts proved to all who witnessed them that the God about whom Paul preached was indeed the true God. Miracles from God authenticated the witness that Jesus is the Savior of all who will believe on Him.

Since the completion of The New Testament, the Bible, in its entirety, is God's standard. We use the Bible to determine the faithfulness of the preacher's message. In Ephesus, God uses Paul to heal and dispel evil spirits who had possessed the bodies of men. It should not astound us that Satan's stronghold responded violently to the invasion of the Gospel of Jesus Christ. Paul would later write to the church at Ephesus instructing them about the believer's spiritual adversary. He wrote

> . . . For we do not wrestle against flesh and blood, but against principalities, against powers, against the rulers of the darkness of this age, against spiritual hosts of wickedness in the heavenly places (Ephesians 6:12).

God brings spiritual salvation to many Ephesians. It resulted in the new believers separating themselves from their idols by burning magical paraphernalia and fetishes used in the worship of their false gods (Acts 19:11-20). When a person receives Christ, there is an inner transformation that shows its change in outward behavior. The new believer's culture and personality will likely determine his outward changes. Change may be dramatic like those from Ephesus or more subtle when the culture he's from is quasi-Christian. In the latter case, a new attitude will likely be the most noted change.

The display of godly teaching and preaching resulted in a major uproar among the citizens, because Ephesus was spiritually a satanic stronghold given over to the worship of the goddess Diana. It was an unruly mob that shouted *Great is Diana of the Ephesians* (Acts 19:35, 35). Disgruntled Ephesians brought Paul and Christian leaders before the Roman Proconsul to answer charges of sedition and disrupting the culture of Ephesus. Presiding officials determined the charges by Jewish instigators were religious in nature and therefore not applicable. Roman law dictated dismissal of the case and the accused freed. The judge ceremoniously dismissed the assembly. Paul remained in Ephesus for an extended amount of time.

Philippi (Acts 20:2-6)

The record is not clear about the sequence of many events but according to Luke's account we next find Paul at Philippi. Because the message was urgent, he sent Titus to Corinth with his letter to act as his emissary and pastoral counsel. He desired that Titus counsel the church about some continued abuses he had addressed in his first letter (2 Corinthians 7:6, 8:6).

Paul, led by the Holy Spirit, journeyed to Greece and remained there for three months and from this location he wrote the book of Romans

(Acts 20:2-3). Scholars consider this letter the definitive word on the doctrine of Justification by Faith (Romans 5:1-6). According to The New Testament record, Paul had never ministered to the church in Rome, but he had heard about their extraordinary faithfulness to Christ (Romans 1:1-7). Now, he writes a letter filled with doctrine outlining man's sinfulness and how both Jews and Gentiles stand condemned before God and how in Christ all men have hope (Romans 10:9,10).

From Greece, Timothy and other brethren went ahead of Paul. Their plan was to meet at Troas where they met, maybe expectantly, seven other brothers (three from Macedonia and four from Asia). These men were likely the ones who were to carry the offering to provide relief to the faithful in Judea (Acts 20:4-6).

Before leaving Corinth for Troas, Paul discovered that a party of adversarial Jews had devised a trap for him at his departure point. He thus altered his plans. He decided to return by retracing his steps through Macedonia. He used this unexpected change in itinerary to encourage the faithful in each city as he retraced his route through Macedonia avoiding Jewish capture.

Troas (Acts 20:7-12)

From Macedonia, Paul made his way to Troas and stayed seven days where on the first day of the week they partook of the Lord's Supper (Acts 20:7-12). These acts of spiritual endearment may hint he is acutely aware of his soon demise. Before leaving, Paul called the disciples together for a final message that lasted until midnight.

The message, energized by so much Truth, provides further evidence Paul was aware he may never see them in this world again. The preaching was so long one young man, sitting in an upper-story window, grew drowsy, went to sleep, and fell to his death. Again, the Lord blessed His people with a supernatural sign of His power by allowing Paul to raise him from the dead (Acts 20:7). The fellowship continued until morning.

Assos and Miletus (Acts 20:13-38)

Leaving Troas, Paul traveled to Assos by foot. The balance of the party left by ship. We are not told why the apostle went over land. We may safely presume it would afford him more opportunities to share his hope in Christ. He rejoined his party in Assos where he boarded the ship. The time for Passover grew near. Therefore, he hurried his journey because he purposed to arrive in Jerusalem for the Passover and to faithfully deliver the relief offering sent from the saints in Macedonia and Achaia.

He continued his journey by sailing to Mitylene, Chios, Samos, Trogyllium, and finally Miletus (Acts 20:13-16). We assume that these were commercial stops to load and unload cargo. There was evidently a planned layover by the ships captain because the party disembarked in Miletus. Paul remained in the port of Miletus, but he sent for the Ephesian elders so he could impress upon them the urgency of faithfully teaching God's Word to the flock. He was greatly concerned about false teachers. Paul warned about these teachers entering the flock like wolves masquerading as sheep. False teaching would corrupt their faith. When he finished his challenging charge he bid them farewell and continued his journey (Acts 20:17-38).

Christianity in every generation would do well to heed Paul's warning. History illustrates, almost without exception, human institutions, despite their noble and righteous beginnings, become corrupt by mixing God's absolute Truth with human reasoning and compromise. Error evolves through mixing the errors of man with the absolutes of God. The Word tells us to: *Trust in the Lord with all thine heart, and Lean not unto thine own understanding* (Proverbs 3:5). Failing to do so results in error. Therefore, when measured against God's absolute Truth, man's work is corrupt if it is not guided by God's unaltered Truth.

Leaders in our churches may come from institutions that no longer believe the Bible or present God as irrelevant. Our churches must concern themselves more with what pastoral candidates believe rather than where they received their education. At one time we could trust a minister who graduated from a certain university or seminary because of its stand on the fundamentals of the faith, however, that day is gone. Even our most trusted institutions can graduate those who merely profess to be Christian. [24]

Beware! Wolves in sheep's clothing are everywhere! They teach in our Sunday schools; they

---

[24] Many educational institutions illustrate the above principle. For example, I recall two nationally known universities, founded in the early years of our country. They originally existed for the sole purpose of training ministers to preach the Gospel of Jesus Christ. These colleges were once bulwarks for defense of God's absolute Truth. However, in today's climate, these same institution's now question more faith than they instill. A friend reported he applied for entrance into the Ph.D. program of one of these institutions. They denied him entrance. Why? Because he believed Adam and Eve were literal people.

write books; they preach from our pulpits; they are in every aspect of Christian service. By observing the fall of secular society into degradation, we may see the enemy increasing his infiltration of our ranks. We may measure Satan's effectiveness by comparing how far the behavior of society deviates from the biblical norm in things like marriage, respect for law, and personal integrity.

As Paul faced the issue of false gods in his culture, so must we face our false gods. We face the various gods of greed, lust, power, covetousness, dishonesty, selfishness, and the like. As with Paul, we must rely on the wisdom of God and the power of His Spirit. While remaining true to the Word, we must avoid the rigidness of legalism; we must adhere to the love and peace of the Spirit while applying the principles of Truth. Remember, we seek to woo the erring brother from his sin. If he will not hear, then he must be lovingly but firmly dealt with from the ground of Truth and expelled from our midst until he shows remorse and evidence of repentance.

Tyre, Caesarea and Jerusalem (Acts 21:1-26)

Leaving Miletus, Paul sailed to Cos, Rhodes, and Patara. The Holy Spirit led in every facet of the journey. The mission party disembarked at Patara and boarded another ship bound for Phoenicia.

Leaving Patara, they sailed to the south side of Cyprus and on to their destination. This ship took them to the large commercial seaport and trade center called Tyre. Their travel by sea terminated there. Luke wrote about Paul and his mission party resting there for seven days (Acts 21:3-6).

Leaving Tyre, they sailed to Ptolemais for one day (Acts 21:7). Luke does not tell us what Paul and his team did while in this fairly small sea port. Because of Paul's intense desire to see people come to Christ, it is easy for us to imagine him engaging people in natural conversation. He did so because God's Truth about the Way of life filled his bosom. During these brief stops on his way to Jerusalem, Paul did not waste time. Undoubtedly, God arranged encounters where His workers planted spiritual seeds of His Word. Paul's energy and love for Christ was such that intuitively he naturally labored to see all who would believe come to Christ.

Leaving Ptolemais, they made their way to Caesarea (Acts 21:8). Paul's party, including Luke and the seven brothers who carried the relief for the Judaea believers, is hosted by Philip the evangelist (Acts 21:8-14). While there, Agabus the prophet, came to Paul and took his belt and bound himself and told Paul he would be bound in like manner if he persisted in going on to Jerusalem. The warning introduced a reminder of the exclamation the Holy Spirit gave Paul when he was converted. God chose him as the apostle to the Gentiles. Speaking of Paul, God had told Ananias . . . *Go thy way: for he is a chosen vessel unto me, to bear my name before the Gentiles, and kings, and the children of Israel: For I will shew him how great things he must suffer for my name's sake* (Acts 9:15, 16).

God had not called Paul to a life of pomp and ceremony. On his way to Jerusalem, he would later meet with certain Roman imprisonment and a sentence of death. It is almost as if the Holy Spirit was reminding Paul that service for God is not without great personal cost.

The principle of self-sacrifice runs throughout the history of God's people. Later, in his epistles, Paul would exhort the church to present themselves as a living sacrifice. He continued to say that doing so was the Christian's reasonable service (Romans 12:1, 2). Man's sinful inclination is to seek others to serve him. But, in contrast, God's Son served man, and then died like a criminal to pay the penalty for man's sin. He did so because, as sinners, we are all under judgment. He promised to save all who believe His witness. God accomplishes this by grace (Ephesians 2:8, 9). When the believer trusts God's message about Christ, God forgives him his sin and takes up residence in his life. Because of the divine nature now residing in him, he is marked by a desire to serve others.

However, these warnings, though well meaning, did not deter Paul from his mission. They served as a test of his commitment to do God's will in the face of personal suffering. Like his Lord, he set his jaw with steel like determination to do the will of the Father. As servants of God, we would do well to resolve, in the power of God's Spirit, to do what we know is the will of the Father for us.

The believers in Jerusalem received the returning mission team with gleeful approval. Excitedly, they shared (1) how in large numbers the Gentiles were believing on Christ, (2) how God was giving victories over the nefarious schemes of unbelieving Jews who were resisting the Gospel, and (3) how many others Jews were faithfully receiving the Word of God in larger numbers. By all measures, Paul and his team had a crowning success on his third missionary journey. Though Luke did not record it, Paul likely had emissaries from the churches in Macedonia and Asia present to James and the elders of Jerusalem the offerings they had gathered for the relief of Judaea.

However, all was not as joyful as earlier thought, because a false report circulated in Jerusalem. Some reported that Paul taught Jews who believed on Christ to abandon their Jewish heritage and no longer follow the laws of Moses. The Christians at Jerusalem knew the report was false, but they had no way of counteracting it without a public demonstration of Paul being faithful, as a Jew, to the traditions of Judaism.

An opportunity came for Paul to prove himself to be a faithful follower of Moses' teaching when James and the Jerusalem elders appealed to Paul to purify himself along with four men who had taken the Nazarite vow.[25] Paul's advisors proposed his action would show his support for the core of Judaism by following the Law given to Moses.

He determined to accompany these men for the ceremony of purification. When they concluded the Nazarite vows, a sacrifice for each man was offered. Paul bore the expenses for the ceremonial sacrifices. By taking such action he hoped to prove, as a follower of Christ, he supported the Law God had given to Moses. The process lasted for a protracted time.

After about seven days, some Jews from Asia recognized Paul as the one they had heard teaching in their home synagogue about Jesus being the Messiah. Upon seeing him, they immediately stirred up the worshippers in the temple. They even claimed Paul had brought a Greek into the temple and by doing so had desecrated the holiness of God. The agitators incited a sense of betrayal of

---

[25] The Nazarite vow is described in Numbers 6:13-21.

God's honor. As a result, an infuriated group of zealous adherents took Paul and charged him with heresy. They began to beat him without mercy. The ruckus caused by the uproar alerted the Roman guards. They came immediately to the point of the attack, broke it up, and arrested Paul. Paul was arrested to protect him from the mob and to allow authorities time to sort out the legalities of the charges (Acts 21:15-26).

Questions for Discussion

1. What was the purpose for the third missionary journey?

2. Name the four major themes in Paul's first Corinthian letter? (It was written during an extended stay in Ephesus.)

3. Paul called for a conference with the Ephesian elders while laying over in Miletus. What was his major concern and how applicable is that concern for our generation?

4. What three major themes were highlighted in Paul's final mission report?

Chapter 7

Paul's
Final Journey

AD 58-68 (Acts 21:27-28:31)

We begin the final journey of Paul's ministry and life by recalling his last arrest in Jerusalem. His arrest came because he believed and taught Jesus of Nazareth was indeed the Jewish Messiah and not for violating Jewish or Roman laws. The Judaizers purposed to kill him when he was discovered in the temple. The mob beating Paul caused a great turmoil. The Roman guards broke up the mob, arrested Paul to protect him and to determine the reason for the uproar.

Paul's Jerusalem Arrest (Acts 21:27-22:29)

After Paul's arrest, the guards began sorting out the reason for the uproar. One commentary stated:

> *The commander, surprised that Paul could speak Greek, had supposed the apostle to be an Egyptian insurrectionist who had not yet been apprehended by the Romans. Evidently this Egyptian rebel was unable or refused to speak Greek.*[26]

In Acts 21:38, we learn the commander of the guard had assumed Paul was a particular Egyptian antagonist who had earlier led four thousand in a failed rebellion against the state. Once Paul, speaking in Greek, explained who he was, he asked for permission to speak to the crowd. Being granted his request, he waited for the crowd's silence.

In your imagination, you can see Paul as he stood on the fortress stairs above the crowd. He began speaking in Hebrew. Many scholars believe he actually spoke in Aramaic which was, in that era, the common language of the Palestinian Jew. This fact does not mean the Bible is in error saying . . . *he spoke to them in Hebrew.* The statement means he spoke in the common dialect used by the Hebrews in that era.

The crowd became more subdued when he spoke in their language. When they heard their beloved Hebrew, the crowd quieted themselves, and he began his defense. He began by explaining his Jewish background. He carefully built his case by

---

[26] Stanley D. Toussaint, *The Bible Knowledge Commentary: An Exposition of the Scriptures*, 1985, 2, 417.

identifying himself as a faithful Jew. He declared his Jewish heritage, including his birth in Tarsus, his tribe as Benjamin and his sect as Pharisee. He continued by stressing his loyalty to Judaism by his desire to destroy all followers of Jesus. He recounted his experience on the Damascus road and how Christ called him to bear a testimony to all men what he had seen and heard. Paul recounted his vision about when Christ appeared to him while worshiping in the temple, warning him he should flee Jerusalem because Jews would not receive his testimony, and instructing him to go to the Gentiles.

When he spoke of the Gentiles, the crowd broke into an uproar calling for Paul's execution. The chief captain of the guard directed that he should be brought into the barracks and flogged.[27] The captain desired to know why the Jews were clamoring for his death. In the midst of these proceedings, Paul declares himself to be a citizen of Rome, and therefore, exempt from being treated as a common criminal without a trial in due process.

Paul Before the Sanhedrin (Acts 22:30-23:10)

Beginning with Acts 22:30, Paul's life seems to rush like molten lava toward the destruction of his personal life. None of his trials took Paul by surprise. The Lord had revealed right after his conversion how great would be his suffering. This suffering did not dampen his spirit. Paul was focused on living by the Lord's teachings and delivering His salvation message of receiving God's grace through faith in Christ.

---

[27] Flogging was a means of punishment and or torture to gain information from unwilling prisoner. Flogging is an act of beating someone with a leather whip.

Upon learning he was Roman, the Captain (desiring to know why the Jews were charging him) released his bonds but held him over until the next day. He then had Paul brought before Priests and the Jewish Sanhedrin.

Before the Sanhedrin, Paul once more sought to prove he was a faithful Jew who had found the Messiah. His remarks infuriated the high priest, who ordered him struck in the mouth for what the priest claimed to be heresy. Paul responded by essentially calling the priest a hypocrite. Being reminded that he had spoken against the high priest, Paul repented and submitted to the priest's authority as the representative of God.

Paul soon realized there were representatives of both the Sadducees and Pharisees present in the council. He used this information to divide the council by declaring himself to be a Pharisee and the son of a Pharisee. The Pharisees, after some discussion, declared there was no guilt in Paul for preaching an angel had appeared to him. Pharisees believed in angels and the Sadducees did not. A heated argument followed when the Pharisees declared him to be innocent of all charges. The contentions became so riotous that Paul was taken by Roman guard into protective custody.

The Assassination Plot (Acts 23:12-23)

Being spiritually blinded by their rage and allegiance to Judaism, the Sadducees sought to seize Paul and execute him immediately. After the Roman guards had extracted him, they set in motion a plot to kill him. Forty of them covenanted together not to eat or drink again until Paul was dead.

Their plan was to have the guards bring him before the council of the Sanhedrin a second time under pretense of further examination. The forty planned to ambush the guards and kill Paul while he was on his way to the council. However, their plot was fouled because Paul's nephew heard them making plans and immediately told Paul.

Paul responded by asking a guard to take his nephew to the chief authority. The guard brought the nephew to the chief captain who took him aside to a private place where he shared the details of the assignation plot. The captain told Paul's nephew not to tell anyone about the plan.

The Roman captain decided to secretly send Paul to Caesarea. He ordered a large party of horsemen and foot soldiers to take Paul to Caesarea to appear before Felix. To avoid attention, they left in the middle of the night. By doing so, they avoided the assassins (Acts 23: 23-25).

Paul Before Governor Felix (Acts 24)

Caesarea, (located northwest of Jerusalem on the Mediterranean Sea) was the provincial headquarters for the Roman governor of Israel and Judea. His name was Felix. The Scripture records that Paul resided in prison for five days before his accusers arrived from Jerusalem, and Felix agreed to hear their claims against him. The priest Ananias and the elders had arranged to have an orator by the name of Tertullus to make their case against Paul.

Tertullus' case comprised four basic charges: Paul was: (1) a pestilent (destructive) fellow (2) a mover of sedition (inciting rebellion) among Jews world wide (3) a ring leader among the sect of the

Nazarenes, and (4) he profaned the temple. The Jews who had accompanied the priests from Jerusalem agreed the charges were true. Having heard their arguments, Felix turns to Paul to hear his response (Acts 24:1-9).

Felix shifted his attention to Paul and asked for his defense. Paul began by referencing his temple experience just twelve days before. He began by saying what he did not do: (1) he did not dispute with anyone in the temple (2) he did not inspire rebellion in the temple or in the city. He then defied anyone to prove the accusations against him were true.

He also confirmed what he did: (1) he confessed that he worshipped God following the way of Jesus which they called heresy (2) he affirmed his belief in the resurrection both the just and unjust (3) he confessed he sought to maintain a conscience without offense to God and man.

He further informed Felix his purpose for being in the temple was twofold: (1) he participated in the rite of purification and (2) he brought alms and offerings to Israel. While worshipping in the temple, certain Jews from Asia (who had experienced his preaching prior to this time) saw him and brought public accusations against him causing a rancor among worshippers (Acts 24:10-18).

Paul continued his defense before Felix by stating that those Asian Jews should have been there to make their charges if they had complaints. However, they were not, and he went on to affirm that had it not been for the disagreement among the accusers over the resurrection of the dead, he would have been released and would not have appeared before the governor's court (Acts 24:19-21).

After hearing Paul's case, Felix commanded Paul's imprisonment until Lysias the chief captain of the Jerusalem garrison could give his witness to what had happened. Felix gave Paul freedom to move about and to receive friends who ministered to his physical needs.

Luke recorded that Felix and his Jewish wife Drusilla called for an interview with Paul. Felix asked about Paul's witness concerning Jesus. The following verses give us pertinent details:

Acts 24-26:

> *24 And after certain days, when Felix came with his wife Drusilla, which was a Jewess, he sent for Paul, and heard him concerning the faith in Christ.*
> *25 And as he reasoned of righteousness, temperance, and judgment to come, Felix trembled, and answered, Go thy way for this time; when I have a convenient season, I will call for thee.*
> *26 He hoped also that money should have been given him of Paul, that he might loose him: wherefore he sent for him the oftener, and communed with him.*

Over the course of two years, Felix interviewed Paul repeatedly and heard his message of God's righteousness, His wrath against sin, and His salvation through the resurrected Christ. Paul's witness had a convicting affect on Felix because he was guilty of many injustices which like ravaging wolves clawed at his heart's door. However, his heart was calloused and would not repent.

It appears the message Paul preached was not his real interest. The backstory suggests Felix had hoped Paul would offer him a bribe to free him.

Bribing officials was apparently a custom of the times. Under certain conditions, a governor could be successfully bribed to release a prisoner. However, Paul persistently offered nothing but God's message of righteous judgment and salvation by grace through faith in Christ.

Paul before Porcius Festus (Acts 25:1-12)

Porcius Festus replaces Felix as the new Roman governor for the province. Upon arrival, he goes up to Jerusalem to confer with the Jewish elders and leaders. This would have been the correct protocol for a governor just beginning his oversight of a province. The wording in the text suggests he met with a larger group than the usual Sanhedrin leadership and leading priests.

Festus desired to get off to a good start with the Jews and therefore he listened carefully to their observations. The report likely contained their view of the state of the province and their suggested solutions. At some point in the deliberations, the high priest requested Paul stand trial in Jerusalem. The nefarious motive for the request was a desire to initiate a second attempt to assassinate Paul enroute. Festus responded that he thought it best to have an initial hearing on the subject upon his return.

Festus remained in Jerusalem another ten days before returning to his residence in Caesarea. A representative body of Jews had accompanied him; they waited for their opportunity to renew their charges against Paul again. The next day Festus had Paul brought into the judgement hall to acquaint himself with the case. The Jews accused as Luke records: . . . *and laid many and grievous complaints against Paul (Acts 25:7).* After hearing the false complaints of the Jews, Festus turned to Paul for his response.

This is what the Scripture says about Paul's reply:

> 8 While he answered for himself, Neither against the law of the Jews, neither against the temple, nor yet against Caesar, have I offended any thing at all.
> 9 But Festus, willing to do the Jews a pleasure, answered Paul, and said, Wilt thou go up to Jerusalem, and there be judged of these things before me?
> 10 Then said Paul, I stand at Caesar's judgment seat, where I ought to be judged: to the Jews have I done no wrong, as thou very well knowest.

Paul did not have a legal representative. He served as his own lawyer. The record indicates Paul addressed Festus only. Paul respectively ignored the presence of Jewish authority. He declared himself innocent of violating either Jewish, Temple, or Caesar's law. When he had finished, Festus asked whether he would be willing to have his case tried in Jerusalem. Paul responded by saying:

> (Acts 25:1-11)
> . . . I stand at Caesar's judgment seat, where I ought to be judged: to the Jews have I done no wrong, as thou very well knowest. For if I be an offender, or have committed any thing worthy of death, I refuse not to die: but if there be none of these things whereof these accuse me, no man may deliver me unto them. I appeal unto Caesar .

Being a Roman citizen, Paul rightly reminded Festus the only proper trial for him was under the jurisdiction of Rome. Festus secretly found no legal reason to hold Paul but for the sake of appeasing the Jews he ignored his defense. However, Paul's appeal to be tried in Caesar's court forced him to follow Roman law. He responds by saying: *Hast thou appealed unto Caesar? Unto Caesar shalt thou go.*

After he had conferred with his council, he determined to send Paul to Rome for a trial before Caesar's court. However, he had to wait for proper travel arrangements. There was no assurance that Paul and the guarding party would safely arrive at their destination. Why? Because, travel in the first century could be dangerous. Robbers by land, pirates by sea, and unpredictable stormy weather made travelers by land and sea vulnerable.

Paul appears before the King (Acts 25:13-26:32)

King Agrippa arrived from Jerusalem to make a courtesy call on the new Roman proconsul. Festus reviewed Paul's case with Agrippa during their greeting and social interactions, In verses thirteen through twenty one, Festus reviews the details of Paul's trial. He informed Agrippa of his dilemma, Festus admitted that under Roman law, Paul was guiltless. However, because Paul had appealed to Caesar, Festus was obliged to follow Roman law granting Paul the rights of a citizen. But, Festus admitted to Agrippa he was having difficulty wording the charges. After hearing the details of the case, Agrippa desired to interview Paul. Festus agrees hoping Agrippa will provide him with a reason to have Paul tried by Caesar. At the appointed time, Agrippa and his sister Bernice are seated in the proconsul's judgment hall and Paul appears before them.

Paul respectfully asserted he had only preached what the Scriptures had prophesied would be Israel's hope. He began with his childhood, his Jewish linage, his training as a Pharisee, his active persecution of Christians whom he believed were heretics, his experience of Jesus on the Damascus road, his healing of blindness caused by the heavenly light, and his commission by Jesus to witness to both Jew and Gentile. Paul starts in verses sixteen and quotes Jesus who said:

> *16 But rise, and stand upon thy feet: for I have appeared unto thee for this purpose, to make thee a minister and a witness both of these things which thou hast seen, and of those things in the which I will appear unto thee;*
> *17 Delivering thee from the people, and from the Gentiles, unto whom now I send thee,*
> *18 To open their eyes, and to turn them from darkness to light, and from the power of Satan unto God, that they may receive forgiveness of sins, and inheritance among them which are sanctified by faith that is in me.*

Paul continued his witness before Agrippa. He shared his message with positive clarity. He declared hope for all who believed God's witness and believed Jesus to be the Christ; to repent of their sin; to prove their repentance by righteous behavior. The apostle insisted he had not preached anything contrary to what Moses and the prophets had foretold about the Christ. He asserted his position stated above was the reason the Jews sought to kill him (Acts 26:1-23).

Near the end of Paul's testimony, Festus interrupted him and said in a loud voice, . . . *Paul thou art beside thyself, much learning doth make thee mad (Acts 26:24b).* Paul denied being mad but asserted he spoke his words in soberness and truth. The court room emptied as Festus and Agrippa conferred about what to do with Paul. They concluded he was not worthy of prison or death. However, because he had appealed to Caesar, Festus must send him to Caesar with full documentation as to why he was sent (Acts 25:13–26:32).

Paul is Sent to Caesar (Acts 27:1-28:16)

Paul and some other prisoners began the journey to Caesar's court in Rome, where Paul hoped to plead his case. Paul and the military escort, under the direction of Julius (a centurion of Augustus' band), booked passage for Julius' prisoners on a boat to Sidon. Though not prisoners, others accompanied Paul on his final journey. Among the passengers were Luke, Aristarchus, and possibly other believers (Acts 27:1-2).

At Sidon, because of Julius' kindness and lenient tendencies, Paul went with friends to refresh himself before putting to sea. It appears, because of difficult winds, the ship sailed along the coast east and north of Cyprus for Myra (Acts 27:3-5). Apparently, the ships, used to navigate their passage were merchant ships doing business as usual.

When they had arrived at Myra, the prison party and other passengers disembarked and sought passage on another vessel patiently making their way to Rome. After some inquiry, Julius found them passage on a ship of Alexandria sailing for

Italy. (This was a larger ship. It held as many as 276 people on board plus huge amounts of grain from Egypt on her way to Rome. Moderns know of these large ships from pictures on the walls of Pompeii and from Lucian's writings, around 150 AD).[28] There was difficulty as they shipped out. A contrary wind made sailing difficult. Progress was slow. A determined captain skillfully sailed the ship along the channel islands. The violent gusts likely caused him to avoid the open sea. The ship, with much difficulty, passed the coastal cities of Cnidus and Rhodes. They continued along a chain of islands and south of Crete to Fair Haven. They were hoping to find a suitable place to harbor for the winter. However, Fair Haven was a bay. If anchored here, the ship would be exposed to the ravages of angry winds upon the open sea (Acts 27:6-8). (J. W. McGarvey, in his commentary on Acts, makes a crucial observation and aids our understanding.[29])

In verse nine of the text, Luke references the celebration of the Passover with the phrase, . . . *after the fast.* The phrase provides us a time reference. The Passover was celebrated in the year of Paul's transport on the 5th of October. Experienced sailors knew from mid-September to the middle of November, the Mediterranean was treacherous. Afterward, the sea was unnavigable for the winter months. Therefore, the pilot

---

[28] Robert James Utley, *Luke the Historian: The Book of Acts*, vol. Volume 3B, Study Guide Commentary Series (Marshall, TX: Bible Lessons International, 2003), 280.

[29] With a favorable wind the boat would have passed to the south of Cyprus; but in tacking to make headway against a contrary wind, they necessarily passed to the east and north-east of that island, leaving it on the left. An additional reason for taking this tack may have been a desire to take advantage of a current which flows westward along the southern shore of Asia Minor, as far as the Archipelago, and greatly favors the progress of westward-bound vessels.

counseled the centurion to allow them to sail about forty miles around the cape of Malta to Phoenicia. Under normal conditions, the ship would have easily negotiated the journey in about seven hours.

Paul, warned by the Holy Spirit, advised the centurion not to set sail. Paul told Julius: *Sirs, I perceive that this voyage will be with hurt and much damage, not only of the lading and ship, but also of our lives* (Acts 27:10).

Julius consulted with the owner and master of the ship. Because their present moorings were insufficient as a winter harbor, the centurion appealed to the ship master to allow a hasty departure for Phoenicia while the winds were favorable.

Paul had warned they should not leave lest they lose the cargo, ship, and possibly their lives. The centurion weighed his options. His commission to deliver the prisoners in a timely manner likely affected his decision. He also felt the experience of the ship's master and the owner carried greater weight than Paul's caution. He granted his approval, and they soon weighed anchor with a strategy to hug the coastline for the forty-mile journey to Phoenicia where they planned to harbor.

Shortly after departure, a fierce northeastern wind of typhoon proportions drove them away from the coast line and out to sea. The Holy Spirit ministered to Paul during the treacherous storm. He assured him nothing would thwart the Father's desire to have him give his witness in Rome.

Paul spoke to the leaders and said:

Acts 27:21-26

21 But after long abstinence Paul stood forth in the midst of them, and said, Sirs, ye should have hearkened unto me, and not have loosed from Crete, and to have gained this harm and loss.
22 And now I exhort you to be of good cheer: for there shall be no loss of any man's life among you, but of the ship.

23 For there stood by me this night the angel of God, whose I am, and whom I serve,
24 Saying, Fear not, Paul; thou must be brought before Caesar: and, lo, God hath given thee all them that sail with thee.
25 Wherefore, sirs, be of good cheer: for I believe God, that it shall be even as it was told me.
26 Howbeit we must be cast upon a certain island.

They were helpless in the sea having no control over the vessel. The ship's master had lost hope of saving the ship. After being tossed about by the sea and blown by the winds for fourteen days, the winds and currents had carried them to the coast of Malta. To lessen the load, the ship's crew had thrown almost everything overboard. Paul warned them to stay with the ship or possibly lose their lives. The fierce winds finally drove them to the place where the two seas met and wrecked them upon the reefs at Malta. The bow became stuck on the reef and the stern was crushed by the turbulent sea. They were at the mercy of God.

The soldiers desired to slay the prisoners lest they escape, but, Julius desired to save Paul and commanded them to abandon ship. All were saved from the disaster. They made their way to shore by either swimming or using pieces of the wrecked ship to buoy themselves in the water (Acts 27:9–28:1).

All passengers, soldiers, prisoners, and sailors survived and gathered themselves on shore. Local residents[30] took mercy on them and cared for them by building a fire and tending their needs. Paul gathered wood for the fire and when he placed the wood on the flames, a venomous serpent recoiled from the fire and lodged its fangs in his flesh. Paul shook himself free of the serpent and showed no ill effects. The natives, who were watching, thought he must be a murderer and thought he had escaped death at sea, justice had finally triumphed. They had expected him to show immediate signs of death. When he showed no ill effects from the venom, they decided he must be a god.

The chief among the peoples was Publius. He courteously hosted them three days. Publius' father was ill as well as others on the island. Through Paul, God healed the island's sick people. Of these events, The Bible Knowledge Commentary has this to say:

> *Publius took Paul and others (us included Luke) to his estate ... for three days. One benefit of Paul's ministry was the healing of Publius' father (who had fever and dysentery) and the rest of the sick on the island. Interestingly Paul, besides not being harmed by the viper, was used by God to heal others. No wonder the islanders honored the shipwrecked men in many ways, even giving*

---

[30] Luke used the term *barbarian* to describe the native islanders. The label was not prejudicial, but simply a term meaning they did not speak Greek.

them supplies before they set sail three months later (v. 11).[31]

The shipwrecked party remained on Malta for three more months before finding passage to Rome on another large commercial vessel of Alexandria that had wintered in the harbor of Malta. The phrase, . . . *whose sign was Castor and Pollux,* was a reference to the dual masthead of the ship representing the patron god's of sailors (Acts 28:2-10).

The Maltese people provided the entire party with a full complement of supplies for the remaining journey. It was probably late February or early March before the final leg of the journey began. The ship sailed for Syracuse, with anticipated stops at Rhegium and Pateoli. There were periods of rest at Syracuse. The ship was in the harbor for three days likely waiting for favorable winds. At Pateoli the ship would unload its cargo, replenish supplies, and take on new cargo for the return trip.

While at Pateoli, Julius allowed Paul to stay with Christian friends. After their days of rest, the soldiers with Paul, his friends, and their other prisoners began the final overland journey. Upon arrival in Rome, the prisoners would likely face one of two fates. They would likely face execution or become candidates for gladiatorial service. Paul was a political prisoner whose fate would be, humanly speaking, determined by Caesar (Acts 28:11-16).

There are many spiritual lessons learned from Paul's journey to Rome. Contemplate several more

---

[31] Stanley D. Toussaint, "Acts," in *The Bible Knowledge Commentary: An Exposition of the Scriptures,* ed. J. F. Walvoord and R. B. Zuck, vol. 2 (Wheaton, IL: Victor Books, 1985), 429.

obvious ones. (1) We may easily perceive Paul had ample opportunities to escape. However, Paul refused these temptations because he knew the Father's will. He was to give his testimony before Caesar. (2) We learn from Paul's behavior during the storm and shipwreck he was at perfect peace knowing he was in God's hands. He knew God would accomplish His sovereign will. (3) When God used Paul as His miraculous instrument of healing, Paul never sought glory for himself but directed glory to God for all accomplishments. (4) The greetings of Roman Christians on his way to Rome encouraged Paul. He was also elated by a second group of Christians meeting him. These are the Christians who had received Paul's letter. It was a letter filled with doctrine that would form the core of the Christian belief system and would guide the Church until Christ comes again. In the midst of all the praise, Paul was reminded that the expressed feeling was the result of God's grace.

Paul is Imprisoned at Rome (Acts 28:11-31)

At Rome, Paul stayed for 2 years under house arrest in his own rented house where he could receive visitors and preach the word (Acts 28: 17-31).

During Paul's extended imprisonment, he wrote a personal letter to Philemon, a prosperous believer, about receiving back an escaped slave whom he had introduced to Christ. He also wrote to churches to which he had earlier ministered. Those receiving an epistle were the Colossians, the Ephesians, and the Philippians.

During these two years Paul was chained to a Roman guard but allowed to lease private quarters and to receive Christian fellowship. For example it appears Luke remained with him through all these trials. Timothy also came to Rome for the express purpose of serving Paul's needs (Colossians 1:1, Phillipians 1:1).

According to Hebrews, Timothy also was in prison at some point during this time (Hebrews 13:23).

Paul, as anticipated, is released around 62 AD from his first Roman imprisonment (Philippians 1:22; 2:19-24). There is no specific Scriptural timeline; there are only statements in various epistles that give us some idea of what his plans might have been.

Between Roman imprisonments, there is a flurry of mission activity. Some suppose Paul succeeds in his desire to go to Spain because he wrote of it when he wrote Romans (Romans 15:28).

Paul went to Crete where he left Titus to work with the church to set up leaders and establish doctrine (Titus 1:5).

He traveled to Miletus and he possibly went to Colossae (2 Timothy 4:20; Philemon 1:22). He met with Timothy in Ephesus and left him there to work with the church to train disciples as he traveled to Macedonia (1 Timothy 1:3). Paul went on to Troas where he left his books and cloak (2 Timothy 4:13).

Paul went to Philippi, where many scholars think he possibly wrote 1 Timothy (Philippians 2:19-24). Some think he wrote the epistle to Titus on his way to Nicopolis where he planned to spend the winter. (Titus 3:12

AD 68 Paul is Executed by Nero

We have no Scriptural record of Paul's death. Actually, Paul was still alive when Luke finished his manuscript about the things the Holy Spirit was doing through the apostles.

Tradition and secular history informs us that, after two years or more being free, Rome issued an order for Paul's final arrest. Nero had seen fit to abandon Roman policy of religious tolerance and launched a crusade to rid the empire of Christians. He made Christians the scapegoat for the burning of Rome. He pursued Christianity with an intense vengeance. In Paul's final imprisonment, Nero denied him the courtesies of house arrest as earlier.

Upon arrival in Rome, the captain of the guard placed Paul in the common prison with serious criminals. Being a professed Christian, made him an enemy of the state, and worthy of despicable treatment reserved for a violent criminal. Being a Roman citizen afforded him some measure of protection from abuse and that his execution would be considered humane.

Somehow he secured writing materials and wrote his final epistle, a second letter to Timothy. In it, he summoned Timothy to come to him, to bring the cloak he had left at Troas, books, and also the parchments. He further asked Timothy to bring Mark with him. He stated that only Luke had remained providing him solace because all others had forsaken him. It appears Paul was feeling the effects from the absence of Christian fellowship (2 Timothy 4:9-12).

Persecution had driven believers out of Rome. Paul's death was eminent. Secular reports indicated that Nero linked Paul with the burning of Rome. Soon after the reading of the charges, guards led Paul, along with other prisoners, outside the city on the Ostian way. They executed Paul by beheading him. Christians who were not Roman citizens were burned at the stake, crucified, or thrown into the lion's den. An early church father, Eusebius, wrote of knowing the burial places (trophies) of both Peter and Paul:

> *But I can show the trophies of the apostles. For if you will go to the Vatican or to the Ostian way, you will find the trophies of those who laid the foundations of this church.*[32]

With the death of Paul, the world possibly lost the most influential man or personality who had a profound affect on Western civilization. The only exception to this statement would be Jesus Christ the God-Man. Though it is obvious, it must be noted only the empowerment of God enabled Paul to accomplish his feats. The God whom the Greek culture knew as the *Unknown God*, we know in the Judeo-Christian culture as Jehovah.

---

[32] Eusebius of Caesarea, Church History Book II Chapter 25:8. www.newadvent.org.

Questions for Discussion

1. What prompted Paul's arrest in Jerusalem and why was he held in protective custody?

2. What defense did Paul offer the mob when he addressed them after being taken into custody and why was he allowed to speak?

3. What was Paul's common defense to both Felix and Agrippa?

4. Why was he sent to Caesar?

5. On what island were they shipwrecked and what miracle gained Paul access to the chief authority on the island?

6.   What route did the prisoners follow on their transport to Rome, and what difficulties were encountered?

7.   What method of execution did Paul suffer and why was he executed in the most humane way known at the time while others suffered crucifixion?

8.   What spiritual lessons did you learn from Paul's final journey?

Chapter 8

Summation
and Application

I discern four major movements in the life of Paul virtually paralleling every generation of believers from Adam and Eve until the end of time: (1) his birth and culture, (2) his encounter with the Savior, (3) his call, and preparation, (4) the exercise of his mission. Consider with me an overview of these and an observation of their spiritual value.

1. Birth and Culture

The Bible affirms God created humans in His image. Therefore, man is not complete until he finds himself at one with God. Like Saul, all people are born into a culture of faith. Your faith system is what you trust in to meet your physical, emotional and spiritual needs.

In the providence of God, Saul of Tarsus was born into the culture of Judaism. His faith system had the true God as its original source.[33] However, when Saul entered life, he was born into a proud Jewish family. He learned about God through a religious system called Judaism. At the time of Saul's birth most of Judaism had fallen into the trap of depending on religion to make them acceptable to God. They had come to promote Judaism's various sects at the expense of God's glory. The Jewish religion focused more on their traditions than the Word of God. Saul did not know God, and the path he followed ultimately served itself. Therefore, as Saul later discovered, he did not serve God, even though he had maintained a life of strict living, and most considered him genuinely religious.

In this present generation, one may be born into a culture of faith based on the system of Truth revealed in the Bible. However, though the Bible is the Word of God, it does not follow that everyone who acknowledges the Bible is at one with God. For example, one may be a member of a Christian church and not know God. Like Saul, many are born into a system of faith based on God's Truth but still not know God.

Since we are all born sinners like Saul, with a nature that naturally gravitates to rebellion against authority, we are separated from God from birth

---

[33] Since God had saved Adam and Eve and taught them to worship him, they in turn taught their children and their children's children taught their children about how to know and worship the true God. However, men like Cain have chosen to worship God in their own way. In doing so, they perverted the way of Truth. Every generation has appended their own perversion to the end that men grope in darkness. Thankfully, God in his mercy is rescuing a remnant of souls from all generations who will believe him. If God had not revealed himself, all mankind would remain eternally separated from God.

(Jeremiah 17:9; Romans 3:23). Under Judaism, Saul had a covenant relationship with God through his parent's faith and the rite of ceremonial circumcision (Genesis 17:9-14). (Because of his parents' faith, he was under the covenant God had made with Abraham.) However, his covenant relationship was only valid until he was cognizant of the reality of God. Then, his salvation was conditioned upon personal faith placed in the promised Messiah who is Jesus. Believing God's testimony has always been the basis of acceptance with God (Romans 4:3; Galatians 3:6; James 2:3).

If you had asked Saul if he knew God, he would have given you a summary of his ethnic and family credentials, his religious affiliations, and his faithful religious activity. This is the same type of response often received in our current generation. When I have the privilege of talking to someone about Christ, I sometimes lead the discussion by asking about their religious heritage. Then, I might ask them to share with me how and when they received Christ. In answering, some unbelievers become very defensive and either claim to have a spiritual background or they do not believe that God exists. They often begin by telling you who their parents are and what station they had in life or the church.

Blinded by their condition, some even claim they have always known God and have never known themselves to be sinners (Romans 3:23). Still, others will offer their church credentials such as when they started Sunday school or when they were baptized as evidence of their conversion. Unknown by them, their answers reveal what they are truly trusting to make them acceptable to God.

Saul had rejected Jesus, God's Messiah; therefore, he was an enemy of God. He proved his commitment to deprecating Christ by agreeing to the stoning of Stephen, Christ's servant, and the persecution of many other Christians. The darkness in Saul's soul left him angry and adversarial. He was not a man at peace! It was in this state we read in the Scriptures of his spiritual awakening on the road to Damascus.

When we are without Christ, our souls are like Saul's, empty and void of true life. We stumble in a maze of sinfulness expressing our fleshly life in more negative and self-centered ways than one can count (Galatians 5:19-21).

2. An Encounter with the Savior

If anyone is to be saved, he must experience an awakening of his soul through the drawing power of the Father's Spirit (John 6:44). It has been the experience of all saved people since Adam's rebellion in the garden. Down through the centuries, the Father has been calling out people for Himself.

One extraordinary day on the road to Damascus, God chose to interrupt the brilliant but self-righteous life of an arrogant Pharisee from Tarsus named Saul. For Saul to be converted to Christianity would be the least likely of all events. It would brand him a Jewish heretic. Yet that is exactly what happened. We covered the event in our consideration of Paul's life. Luke carefully recorded it in his detailed report of the *Acts of the Apostles* (Acts 9:1-19). His conversion was referenced and repeatedly shared by Saul as well as others.

After his salvation, Saul began using his Roman name Paul (Acts 22:1-16; 26:9-18).

The number of times Paul shared his story is an indication of how important it is for believers to share their spiritual story. The story of how God granted you mercy and forgave your personal sins is unique to you. Like Paul, we must show God's willingness to grant grace to those who receive His Son as personal Lord. God can only grant grace because Jesus paid for the sins of the world with His death on Calvary (John 1:29). In effect, Jesus became the believing sinner's substitute.

You and I may not have been startled by a brilliant light like Paul, but each has known what it means to be awakened to our personal sinfulness, to need forgiveness, and to not know where to receive it. In His mercy God brought His message into your life. God may have used a friend sharing his story, a Gospel tract, a Bible teacher, a preacher, or simply giving you a spiritual awareness, He awakened you to the fact you are accountable to Him and you have no defense against His charges.

When the awakening comes, whether over time or all of a sudden, we intuitively know we must respond. Some eagerly repent, while others go into denial. They refuse to admit their lostness and need for God. Then there are others who acknowledge the need, but refuse to act because they somehow believe Satan's lie that the offer of salvation is open-ended. Why is it a lie? Because, Isaiah said: *Seek ye the Lord while he may be found, Call ye upon him while he is near* (Isaiah 55:6). The clear implication is God is only available when He makes you aware of His nearness.

Like Abraham, Saul was counted righteous when he believed God. His act of faith began the initial phase of salvation called justification. Likewise, when we believe what God said Jesus did for us, repent of our sins, and receive His forgiveness, we are counted just before the Lord. This is what happens: God takes the righteousness of His Son and applies it to the believing sinner so (for the sake of Christ) he is counted as one who had never sinned.

Those who receive the offer of mercy through faith in Christ are *justified,* and begin the second part of the salvation process.

3. The Call and Preparation

Immediately after his submission to Christ, Paul desired to know what Christ would have him do (Acts 9:6). It is the most natural of all processes. But, what few realize is God wants us to *be* before we *do*.

The process of being a Christian is a lifetime vocation. It begins the moment we say yes to Christ and it does not end until we arrive in heaven. In theology, the daily process of being a Christian is called *sanctification*. It means to be set apart for God's use. It is not an event, so much as a process. In Paul's case, it meant Paul was no longer his own man. He was under new management. Judaism no longer had a hold on him. He was now free to be at the beckoned call of his new Master, the Lord Jesus Christ. His standard of availability was to be on call moment by moment.

What was true of Paul is true of every person who receives Christ. In the same manner, when we yield ourselves to Christ's love, we come under new management. From the moment we believe on Christ, we are positionally set apart for God's immediate use, and He begins the process of making us into the likeness of Jesus (Hebrews 13:19, 20).

Believers become slaves of love, not fleshly lust, but a godly love as in a parents' love for a child or more appropriately God's love for us (John 3:16; 1 Corinthians 15:3). As family members, God directs His love toward us. He loved us before as part of His creation. But now we become the objects of His love in in a different way. Why? Because, we are now family. The love of God often shows itself in our being disciplined (Hebrews 12:5, 6). Sometimes He allows us to face suffering because we have identified ourselves with Him or because there are lessons we need to learn about life (Acts 9:15, 16). The world hates God and it will also hate us (John 7:7).

The Lord took Paul aside for an extensive period of training and reflection. He then took him on three missionary journeys where he learned to apply the Truth and principles he had been taught. In like manner the Lord trains us (2 Timothy 2:2).

4. A Sense of Personal Mission

The Lord continues to prepare us as we serve Him. Our training never ends! Our service for God continually shows us the intricacies of our relationship to Him and His Glory in our lives.

God bestows spiritual gifts for the express benefit of serving others. Therefore, the believer must utilize his gift(s) in personal ministry as directed by the Spirit. Every Christian has at least one spiritual gift bestowed upon him by the Holy

Spirit. This gift (or gifts) is given for the benefit of other Christians (Romans 12; 1 Corinthians 12; Ephesians 4:7-12).

One of the most disappointing things we observe in the modern church is the false idea about who may render ministry. People commonly think only pastors, or other vocationally called ministers may effectively serve God. This is one of Satan's boldest lies! Every believer has both the privilege and responsibility to engage in the ministry of Christ by serving others. You may begin, even now, by following the Holy Spirit's leading.

If you have an area of genuine concern, it is likely the Lord is calling you to work in that very area. If you cannot get the church interested in your particular concern, just start by yourself. Use your own resources as the Lord provides. In this manner, I remember one lady who started a weekly Bible study for children in one of our city's housing projects. Ashamedly, it was not a church ministry vision. However, it was a vision of the Spirit, and He used her successfully for years. Thankfully the church did finally provide her with some physical resources to help in the ministry.

Christian, find out what God wants you to do and do it! As Henry Blackaby would say: *Find out what God's doing and get in on it.* In charging you in this way, I do not mean you should circumvent the local church where you attend. Your pastor is charged with the task of leading your congregation in reaching your community and teaching you how to minister to one another in the church. However, as the Spirit leads, do not limit your ministry to church mission projects. God may give you a personal burden to meet a particular need. If so, He desires to give you the joy of serving Him in meeting that need. Obey Him by following His leadership and you will be richly blessed.

In His providence, God used Nero as an instrument to bring Paul into his final phase of salvation. It is the phase called *glorification*. It is thus called because when Jesus rose from the dead He received a glorified body. We believe it is such a body we will possess throughout eternity. It is a physical body with supernatural characteristics. In this state, one truly knows the reality of eternal salvation with God.

There is a sense in which the four phases of Paul's life become a microcosm of God's plan for the ages. Jehovah has revealed His ultimate purpose through His Word. His purpose is the restoration of His creation. Since the fall of Adam and Eve, God has been at work weaving the affairs of redeemed people into the fabric of His purpose. Ultimately, His work will lead to a new heaven and a new earth (Revelation 21:1-6).

What will we be doing in heaven? I am convinced all eternity will find us engaged in worshipping Him, learning about Him, and ministering to Him. Although God is self-sufficient and needs nothing, He enjoys the praise of His people who worship Him for who He is. Furthermore, I believe our learning about the character, holiness, righteousness, purity, and mercy of our God will enthrall us and everything learned will hold us in wonder.

Awaiting us in heaven will be an adventure greater than the sum of all our imaginations!

PART TWO

THE MYSTERIES
OF GOD

. . . according to the revelation
of the mystery, (Romans 16:25b)

The hidden things of God
are mountain peaks of Truth
that enhance and sustain
the children of God.

Chapter 1

Explaining the Mysteries

(The Hidden Things of God)

I invite you to join me as I embark upon a discovery of these mountain peaks of Truth. These are the secrets our Lord Jesus taught Paul. The hidden mysteries were in the His heart until the very moment Christ called Paul into Arabia.

Paul was there for approximately three years in what I would call a reflective retreat. The Lord Jesus taught him about specific spiritual realities he calls mysteries. These mysteries are mentioned by Paul in numerous places in his epistles and are crucial to understanding the Christian life. These Truths tell us how Christians shall live and function in a world that God will ultimately recover for His own glory (Revelation 21:1).

The mysteries or secrets revealed to Paul are like mountain peaks of Truth rising above all previous revelations. In God's progressive nature of revealing Himself, new Truth does not negate the importance of earlier revealed Truth. When God shares, we observe His shared Truth line upon line and precept upon precept.

One analogy would be to view yourself taking a trip from the lowlands to the mountains. There is a gradual rise from the lowlands to the rolling hills, to the smaller mountains, and then to the grand towering peaks.

We recently took a brief mini-vacation to North Carolina's Blowing Rock. While there, we took several trips on the Blue Ridge Parkway. We stopped along the way at overlooks where we viewed vistas of the valleys and other mountain peaks showcasing God's majestic beauty in creation. This analogy helps me view God's Truth as an unfolding landscape. All Truth is vitally important in accomplishing God's purpose. However, as one Truth builds upon another, God's ultimate purpose becomes clear.

God's most majestic mountain peak of Truth is the revelation of His Son as the Savior of the world (Ephesians 1:10). The secrets shared with Paul mostly had to do with the Church, who she is, how she is to worship, what her position is in heaven, and how she is to function in the world. Paul alludes to the Church as The Bride of Christ, and she is to magnify the presence of the groom (Revelation 21:9). These shared Pauline teachings reveal the position and the hope of the Church made up of individual believers from all congregations.

The experiential realities of living the Christian life are taught in these mysteries. Understanding them better will assist us in discharging our commission to teach them to others (2 Timothy 2:2).

We begin with a phrase found in Paul's letter to the Romans:

> *Romans 16:25*
> *Now unto him that is of power to establish you according to my gospel, and the preaching of Jesus Christ, according to the revelation of the mystery, which was kept a secret since the world began.*

The Greek word translated *mystery* has a different application in Greek than its common usage in English. When we speak of a *mystery* (in English), we are referring to a puzzle or something we must solve using our rational powers. However, when God uses the word *mystery*, He is referencing something that He has chosen to keep secret until a specific moment in our time. Therefore, God's mysteries are His secrets not yet revealed. Know this: if God were not willing to reveal His secrets, we would not uncover them on our own. This would not happen even if we had all the world's accumulated wisdom. Therefore, we must depend on His revealing His secrets as it pleases Him to do so.

Remember, God's revelation of His eternal plan is progressive in nature. For evidence of this fact, consider man's condition when God placed Adam and Eve in the garden in Eden. He did not reveal to them everything about Himself. It appears that they were on a need to know basis. We do not know how much information He shared, but He clearly did not share everything. All we know is God was in fellowship with them daily, and He warned them of the dangerous consequences of eating from the fruit of the tree of Good and Evil (Genesis 2:16, 17).

Therefore, beginning with Adam, God has progressively revealed Himself and His purposes to all men generally, and specifically to those who have believed Him. For example, if we were using a scale of one to ten, Adam and Eve were probably at one-to-three on the *revelation scale* while today's Christian is on the other end at ten. God does not reveal to us why He did not inform our first parents of all He had planned.

The Scripture says . . . *In the fullness of time, God sent forth His Son into the world.* This phrase testifies about Christ being God's final revelation of Himself and His deliberate plan for the ages (Galatians 4:4; Ephesians 1:10). From the Son's revelation, we understand the Father's ultimate purpose for three major people groups: Israel, the Gentile nations, and the Church.

Only through the Son did the Father reveal these specific hidden teachings. The Lord Jesus taught some to the first apostles. However, there were yet other things they were not ready to hear. After Paul's conversion, the resurrected Christ, met with Paul for an extended time in Arabia where He revealed the balance of these secrets. Now the Word, from God to man, is complete. There are no other secrets He wishes to reveal until we arrive in Heaven because, He said . . . *we know that, when he shall appear, we shall be like him; for we shall see him as he is.* To be in His presence in that dimension is to have knowledge beyond our present capacity.

We introduce the subject of God's secrets by referencing Paul's closing benediction in his letter to the Romans.

Romans 16:25-27

25 Now to him that is of power to stablish you according to my gospel, and the preaching of Jesus Christ, according to the revelation of the mystery, which was kept secret since the world began,
26 but now is made manifest, and by the scriptures of the prophets, according to the commandment of the everlasting God, made known to all nations for the obedience of faith:
27 to God only wise, be glory through Jesus Christ for ever. Amen. (Emphasis mine)

Focus on verse twenty-five. The word *power* speaks of God's sufficient ability to begin our relationship with Him and to sustain it. Paul is here stressing the reality of the Father's ability to establish believers in *the faith*. Paul's message is God's Word, and the power of the Word establishes believers as members of God's family. The experience is not a magical one but rather *supernatural*. God in His mercy, performs a supernatural work of grace in the life of the believer and the believer is never the same. Grace comes as a newly created life residing in the spirit of the new believer. This newly created life is sustained and maintained by God the Holy Spirit.

Paul's preaching that Jesus Christ is the Lamb of God who died for us, was buried for us, is now raised for us, and is victorious over sin for us, is a message that establishes us in God's family forever. The Father reveals Jesus as the source of His grace, and He bestows mercies to all who trustingly believe in Him. What are we to believe? We must believe His witness about Himself in His Word!

The propagation of Paul's infectious message is the power of God unto salvation (Romans 1:16). The salvation message of grace through faith procures justification before God forever (Ephesians 2:8,9). But the Truth delivered by Jesus to Paul in Arabia provided a greater understanding of both the Gospel's nature and its benefits. It is not a matter of just intellectually embracing facts, but rather investing one's heart in the will of Him who created all things.

When God sent forth His Son, He revealed through Him the mysteries held in His bosom from the beginning of time. The secrets were about the spiritual realities experienced by members of His body (the Church). He revealed these realities to Paul and he became the channel through whom the Holy Spirit disclosed these secrets for the Christian's edification. His purpose for revealing them is found in verse twenty six: . . . *for the obedience of faith* (Romans 16:26). One may be assured that all of the Father's communication with man is designed for our worshipping Him, obeying Him, and understanding His purposes.

But, I remind you again, God's revelation is progressive. During His earthly or pre-crucifixion ministry, Jesus shared with His disciples what they needed to know for the completion of their *pre-crucifixion mission*. Jesus' initial ministry was almost exclusively directed to the house of Israel.[34] He presented Himself to Israel as their promised Messiah. Then, in preparation for His *post-crucifixion ministry*, He alluded to the Church

---

[34] While focusing His ministry on Israel, Jesus also touched the lives of believing Gentiles.

but did not provide details (Matthew 16:17,18). Why? Possibly, because His disciples would have been confused by their present Jewish identity. There was no place for the Gentile nations in the theological thinking of the Jews. Except for some Gentile proselytes, the Jews considered the Gentile nations a lost cause, and an alienated people under the curse of God.

In Acts, Luke records an event where God appeared to Peter in a vision. The vision startled Peter and caused him to re-evaluate all God had previously demanded of him. Until this time, the Jews had been taught that to have anything to do with Gentiles would cause them to be unclean and in need of spiritual cleansing. Through the vision at Joppa, God made it clear to Peter He was opening His message to believing Gentiles.

While God was dealing with Peter in a vision, He also used a vision to inform a Gentile named Cornelius about Peter. Cornelius, a Roman centurion searching for God, was told in a dream to send for Peter (Acts 10). The unfolding of these visions in actual life experience shows us the heart of God for all people who seek Him.[35]

It was during His post-resurrection ministry that Jesus called Paul and commissioned him as His final apostle (Acts 9:15). Paul's mission was to prove to the Jews, from the Old Testament Scriptures, Jesus was God indwelling human flesh and as such was their promised Messiah. His message to the Gentiles was Jesus is the Savior of all who will trustingly believe on Him (Acts 16:30, 31). Paul based his witness to the Gentiles on the

---

[35] In Acts 10, God introduces the fact that He accepts all Gentiles who will believe His message. Even in the Old Testament God saved Gentiles who believed Him. Examples: Nineveh, Ruth, and Rahab.

fact that (1) Jesus was and is the Son of God, (2) He was sent from God to bear the sin of the world, and (3) He rose from the dead proving Himself victorious over the power of sin and the curse of spiritual and physical death (1 Corinthians 15:1-3).

The Truth Jesus witnessed to Paul is now fully and plainly revealed in his New Testament epistles. All revelation from God has now ended! Therefore, faith in the Son's witness will bring salvation to believers and glory to the only-wise God.

In the following chapters we discover the secrets given to Paul. These secrets are teachings that primarily focus on the Church. Paul informs us about the Church and how she is to function and worship in a fallen world. He reveals Christ's Church as the spiritual Body of Christ (John 3:29, Revelation 21:2, 22:17). The Church as an entity was not known nor witnessed to in the Old Testament.

After studying Paul's life, let us give our attention to the secrets of God. While the hidden secrets of God were made known to Paul alone, they were confirmed by the other apostles (1 Peter 3:15,16). Our study of Paul's witness to the *secrets* in his epistles will unfold in the following manner. Each of the seven major secrets considered is dealt with separately looking at each using the following topics:

Explanation: The purpose is to determine the historical and cultural setting of each secret.

Exposition: Here we seek to discover the content of the text and its teaching.

Exhortation: In this section we desire to encourage believers to obediently respond to the teaching and its application for today.

Questions for Discussion

1. What does the Greek word translated *mystery* mean?

2. What is progressive revelation?

3. Define:

    a. Pre-crucifixion ministry

    b. Post-resurrection ministry

4. What is meant by the term Body of Christ?

5. List and describe the three topics under which the mysteries are studied.

Chapter 2

The Mystery Of God (The Trinity)

In the beginning God . . .

(Genesis 1:1a)

For by him were all things created, that are in heaven, and that are in earth, visible and invisible, whether they be thrones, or dominions, or principalities, or powers: all things were created by him, and for him: 17 And he is before all things, and by him all things consist.

(Colossians 1:16, 17)

The above texts would be laughed at and scorned were they to be read in a secular academic setting. Why? Because the natural or unbelieving man does not receive the witness of the Spirit (1 Corinthians 2:14).

The subject of God has been a troubling concept for man. Philosophers, scientists, and theologians have debated for centuries about whether or not God exists, about the origins of life, and how the earth, planets, galaxies, and universes were formed. Many set forth exotic theories seeking to answer the questions that haunt mankind.

For example, scientists with their scientific method and philosophers with their rationalistic logic continue to claim they are making advances in resolving the questions about how life originated. Mean while, many highly acclaimed archeologists continue to affirm the accuracy of the biblical account of man's history, thus causing a potential dilemma.

Ever since man disobeyed God in the garden, there has been a propensity for sinful man to find answers for himself instead of relying on the witness of God. Nevertheless, Jehovah has been faithful to provide a witness to His Truth in every generation. Although God's revelation of Himself has been progressive, the way of man's salvation has always been the same: trustingly believe God and be saved.

At the end of the Old Testament, God had not fully revealed His purposes for the ages. There were yet some essential Truths He desired to share. In this chapter, we consider one Truth Paul would never have believed had it not been for the witness of Jesus. Therefore as we contemplate the content of our text, be sensitive to the witness of the Spirit to your own heart.

Explanation

Our text reminds us that God created all things. How do we know? We know because it is the testimony of God's Word. We make no apologies for basing our faith on the authority of God's witness. The Bible is our final authority because God was the only one present at creation. Only He is capable of providing us with what we need to know and believe about life and eternity.

Neither science, natural religion or philosophy can provide definitive answers about God, creation, and the meaning of life. Only our creator has accurate answers and He has revealed them to us in His Word *The Holy Bible*.

Man inherently has a need to know from where he came, why he is here, what is his purpose, and what will happen to him when he dies. All religions try to answer these questions, but only the Bible provides us authoritative answers. Why? Only God is qualified to provide answers about life. The witness of the Bible is based on the teachings of the Father who sent His Word through prophets. His Son Jesus was His final witness. When Jesus rose from the dead He proved Himself victorious over death, sin, and the devil. Therefore, because He conquered death, He alone has authority to provide answers about life.

The concept of God was not a new revelation to Saul. From the days of Abraham and Moses, his forefathers taught Israel to worship and serve the one true God Jehovah. The prophets had faithfully recorded the Word from Jehovah, and the tribes of

Israel had passed on His teachings from generation to generation.

When Saul met Jesus on the Damascus road, he was startled by the sudden confrontation. Why? Because he had thought himself God's faithful servant. He felt more than justified in pursuing the followers of Jesus because he thought them to be heretics of the grossest sort.

Why do you suppose he was startled? May I suggest two possible reasons: (1) perhaps Saul had never had a supernatural contact with God and therefore the sudden encounter was a foreign experience; (2) Saul's preconceived ideas about God did not include the possibility of God incarnating Himself in human flesh. Saul of Tarsus had known nothing of the threefold personalities of God before Jesus taught him.

The following exposition on the Trinity is in keeping with the three persons of the God-Head being equal in power, authority, and nature. The illustration below will help in understanding God being three-in-one. The mystery lies in the fact that there is only one God who reveals Himself in three divine persons.[36]

Remember, the Father is not the Son and the Father is not Spirit; the Son is

---

36 The chart illustrating the Trinity is my rendition, but I am not the originator. We are indebted to the original designer whoever that may be.

not the Father and the Son is not the Spirit. The Spirit is not Father, the Spirit is not the Son. However, the Father is God, the Son is God and the Spirit is God. It is easier to understand their functionality than their all being one as God. Orthodox Christianity is monotheistic, meaning we worship one God even though our critics refuse to recognize our Christian monotheism claiming we worship three Gods.

Exposition

According to Colossians 1:17, the Son of God is self-existing. Therefore, He existed before all things which indicates He is co-eternal with the Father. By Him all things have come to exist, and continue to exist.

Our two primary texts deal with God and creation. We are focusing on what Saul (now called Paul) learned from Jesus about God. This information had only been partially revealed to the other apostles.

Paul's concept of God radically changed after he met Jesus on the Damascus road. When he had previously seen the Lord on the streets of Jerusalem, he saw no more or less a gifted but a mild-mannered teacher who had great influence over the common people. Nevertheless, on the Damascus road, he met the majestic King in all the brilliance of His essence.

Prior to this experience, Paul had only known the invisible God through Israel's storied tradition and history. God was real to him through the stories shared by his parents and in his formal training at Gamaliel's feet. However, he may have never had a personal relationship with God as did the likes of Mary, Joseph, Simeon, and Elizabeth (mother of John the Baptist). His concept of God had likely been a cold scholastic view gained through meticulous and tedious study of the Law or the word of God through the teaching of Moses.

As Jesus taught him in Arabia, a new understanding of God's nature began to settle upon his consciousness. He began to understand the secret that God would have him teach about God's being. He learned it was Jesus who created all things under the authority of His Father and in the power of His Spirit. This marvelous Truth about God had been hinted about in the Scriptures, but was now clearly apprehended by Paul, and he wrote of it in his letter to the Colossians (Colossians 1:16, 17).[37]

From this text we learn several things: (1) Jesus Christ is the Son of God and as such is deity, (2) Jesus created all things including the angels, and (3) His very existence holds all things created together.

God must have exercised divine patience as Paul processed what he had never known or contemplated prior to the mysterious but divine light on the Damascus road. God introduced him to the reality of God's nature being three-in-one.

At some point in the Lord's tutoring him, it dawned upon his consciousness that the Father created all things through His Son in the power of His Spirit. This was one of the mysteries or secrets of God that Paul learned from Jesus in Arabia.

---

[37] The functional submissive relationship of the Son to the Father and the Spirit to the Son does not mean they are not equal in authority, attributes and nature.

Exhortation

The concept of God being one in three persons is known as the doctrine of the *Trinity*. The word *trinity* is nowhere mentioned in the Bible. However, evidence of its reality is found in both the Old and New Testaments on multiple occasions.

For example, when God recorded the creation of man he hinted at there being a plurality in the God-Head in Genesis 1:23 . . . *God said, Let us make man in our image, after our likeness:* . . . Take note of the phrase *let us*. The phrase suggests more than one. Again, we see in Genesis 11:7 . . . *Go to, let us go down, and there confound their language, that they may not understand one another's speech.*

The context is the building of the Tower of Babel.

We find another possible example in Genesis 18:

Genesis 18:1-3

1And the Lord appeared unto him in the plains of Mamre: and he sat in the tent door in the heat of the day;
2 And he lift up his eyes and looked, and, lo, three men stood by him: and when he saw them, he ran to meet them from the tent door, and bowed himself toward the ground,
3 And said, My Lord, if now I have found favour in thy sight, pass not away, I pray thee, from thy servant:

The passage above is thought by many an example of a *theophany*. A theophany is a physical manifestation of God. In this case, we have God: the angel of the Lord appearing to Abram as three men. It is thought the three men represent God the Father, God the Son, and God the Holy Spirit.

In the New Testament there are a number of passages where one may observe the activity of all three of the persons of the God-Head in one verse. Here are some examples:

> Luke 4:18,19
> 18 The _Spirit_ of the Lord is upon _me_, because _he_ hath anointed _me_ to preach the gospel to the poor; _he_ hath sent _me_ to heal the brokenhearted, to preach deliverance to the captives, and recovering of sight to the blind, to set at liberty them that are bruised,
> 19 To preach the acceptable year of the Lord.

One may observe Jesus speaking (me), the Spirit anointing Him, and the Father (he) sending Him on mission.

> John 3:5
> _Jesus_ answered, Verily, verily, _I_ say unto thee, Except a man be born of water and of the _Spirit_, he cannot enter into the kingdom of _God_.

Jesus the Son is speaking, He is referencing the Spirit, and the subject is the Father's kingdom. Therefore, all three persons of the God-Head are actively participating.

> Romans 8:11
> But if the _Spirit_ of him that raised up _Jesus_ from the dead dwell in you, _he_ that raised up _Christ_ from the dead shall also quicken your mortal bodies by _his Spirit_ that dwelleth in you.

The word _Spirit_ refers to the Holy Spirit; the pronouns _He_ and _His_ refer to the Father, and the names _Jesus_ and _Christ_ are the Son of God.

Ephesians 2:18
For through <u>him</u> we both have access by one
<u>Spirit</u> unto the <u>Father</u>.

In the context, the pronoun *Him* is Christ the Son, the word *Spirit* is the Holy Spirit, and *Father* references God the Father.

Hebrews 9:14
How much more shall the blood of <u>Christ</u>, who
through the eternal <u>Spirit</u> offered <u>himself</u>
without spot to <u>God</u>, purge your conscience
from dead works to serve the living <u>God</u>?

The phrase *the blood of Christ* and the pronoun *himself* speaks of the Son of God, the *Spirit* is the Holy Spirit and the term *God* is God the Father.

One cannot deny the teaching about the trinitarian God-Head revealed to Paul and through him to the other apostles. Why? Because, its precept is repeated in most if not in every Pauline epistle. Therefore, because Paul had a profound effect on all the writers of The New Testament, it is easy to see why they too included the precept in their writings.[38]

If the historians are correct, no New Testament book existed for at least fifteen years after Paul's retreat with Jesus in Arabia. It is thus likely Paul's teaching permeated all streams of Christian witness. All apostles endorsed the concept of one God showing Himself in three persons. It is truly a mystery difficult for the human mind to dissect, but one that is essential to the Christian message.

God the Father is Holy and righteous; He cannot tolerate sin in any measure; He cannot

---

[38] Peter, the acknowledged head of the apostles, gave full affirmation to the writings of Paul in 2 Peter 3:15, 16.

excuse sin. Sin has robbed God of His glory and His fellowship with His creation. Mankind is under the curse of sin. If there is to be redemption and restoration of glory, God Himself must offer a sacrifice for all sins past, present, and future. Why God? Because, only God is holy, righteous, and sufficient to make an adequate sacrifice to satisfy His own standard of holiness.

In eternity past, God the Son offered Himself to be the sacrifice to restore the Father's glory and bring eternal peace and redemption from God's wrath on sin for all who received the Son. The Father sovereignly pronounced it would be so, thereby sealing the names of believers in the book of Life and sealed the fate of the crucified Lamb even before the foundation of the world (Revelation 13:8).

In the fullness of time, the plan successfully unfolded in human history; the Son died a cruel death at the hands of sinners; He was buried and on the third day arose from the dead by the power of the Spirit. He was victorious over all that had robbed God of His glory and His sacrifice has guaranteed His creation will see complete restoration of His glory.

Praise Father, Son, and Holy Ghost!

Questions for Discussion

1. When Paul discovered Jesus created all things, he became aware of the plurality of the God-Head. True or False? Why have you given your answer?

2. What is the doctrine of the Trinity?

3. How many God's do Christian's worship? Why have you given your answer?

4. Name the three persons of the God-Head and discuss the primary function of each.

Chapter 3

The Mystery
Of The Faith

Holding the mystery of the faith in a pure conscience. (1 Timothy 3:9)

Explanation

In Paul's first letter to Timothy, he was introducing the importance of viewing God's revelation as a complete body of Truth. At this juncture in history, Christian doctrine such as the Apostle's Creed did not exist.[39] However, several teachings on various issues had already been

---

[39] Doctrines of faith were likely not written in a formal statement until the completion of the New Testament canon. The first mention of the Apostle's Creed was in 390 AD.

shared and more would follow. Paul realized it would be important to communicate to his leaders and those who followed that these teachings would ultimately form a body of particular Truth and that these teachings must be systematically shared with all believers.

As Paul mentored Timothy, he taught him what Christ had shared about the Church and its members. Here is a list of the type things he taught:

1. What they must believe.

2. How they must live.

3. How they must worship.

4. What leadership they must follow.

5. How they must relate to leaders such as pastors, etc.

6. How they must treat one another,

7. What their mission must be in the world.

Paul gradually taught his proteges about each of these areas.

Out of the above context Paul emphasizes two essentials regarding Truth as a whole unit: (1) what we are to hold: *the mystery of the faith,* and (2) how we are to hold it: *with a pure conscience.* Consider these essentials in their chronological order.

Exposition

The Faith is not only a body of divine teaching revealed by God and entrusted to believers, it also includes an act of dependence on that particular body of teaching. Paul's teaching began with the Gospel, but it embodied much more than the facts necessary for salvation. His teaching sets forth a body of heavenly Truth that includes all the Son of God shared in that spiritually intimate time in Arabia. Once you apprehend the Truth it must be held fast in your spirit without mental reservations.

It is somewhat common for people to affirm something with which they do not really agree. How do they justify that type of action? They do so by reinterpreting (or rationalizing) the meaning of their agreement. For example, if one were asked to sign a document declaring the Bible is the Word of God, some people may readily sign it even if they believe the Bible *only contains a portion of the Word of God*. However, such action would violate the conscience of those who accept the Bible and its message at face value.

The Bible is not a book based on human opinions, but it is vital revelation from God. It is God's good news entrusted to Christians as the very oracles of the living God. In Old Testament history, these oracles came through the prophets and holy men chosen by God to convey His principles to those who believed in Him and trusted their future to Him.

In The New Testament era and beyond, God has made Himself known through His Son. The fullest revelation of God known to mankind is Jesus Christ. When we look at Christ, we see what God is like. We know this because of the witness given to us in His Word. It clearly testifies Jesus is God in the flesh.

The writer of the book of Hebrews, whom some teachers think was Paul, made it clear when he wrote under inspiration of the Spirit:

Hebrews 1:5-8

5 For unto which of the angels said he at any time, Thou art my Son, this day have I begotten thee? And again, I will be to him a Father, and he shall be to me a Son?
6 And again, when he bringeth in the first begotten into the world, he saith, And let all the angels of God worship him.
7 And of the angels he saith, Who maketh his angels spirits, and his ministers a flame of fire.
8 But unto the Son he saith, Thy throne, O God, is for ever and ever: a sceptre of righteousness is the sceptre of thy kingdom.

With the first twelve apostles Christ primarily directed His mission to the nation of Israel. He taught them what they needed to know while laying the groundwork for introducing and building His Church. The Church, as a body, was given for the completion of Christ's mission in the world. After Christ completed His primary mission of dying for the sins of the world, He unveiled the Father's secret about the Church. The Church would be called the Bride of Christ.

The Lord Jesus gave His first apostles hints about the Church so they would know when they heard about it in the future. So when Paul declared the teachings revealed to him by Jesus, the other apostles recognized the revelation to be true and faithful to all Jesus had taught them. We know this because of Peter's counsel in 2 Peter 3:13-17.

Observe carefully what Peter says about Paul and his writings in:

2 Peter 3:13-17
13 Nevertheless we, according to his promise,

look for new heavens and a new earth,
wherein dwelleth righteousness.
14 Wherefore, beloved, seeing that ye look for
such things, be diligent that ye may be found
of him in peace, without spot, and blameless.
15 And account that the longsuffering of our
Lord is salvation; even as our beloved brother
Paul also according to the wisdom given unto
him hath written unto you;
16 As also in all his epistles, speaking in them
of these things; in which are some things hard
to be understood, which they that are
unlearned and unstable wrest, as they do also
the other scriptures, unto their own
destruction.
17 Ye therefore, beloved, seeing ye know
these things before, beware lest ye also, being
led away with the error of the wicked, fall
from your own stedfastness.

Notice verses 15 and 16 in the above passage. Peter is clearly endorsing Paul's teaching as revelation from God. Peter, as the recognized leader among the first twelve apostles, affirms the teaching of the last apostle. This is a crucial point lest we fall into the trap of treating one apostle's teaching as superior to another's. It cannot be emphasized enough: All of God's Word has equal authority but understood progressively. Therefore, we understand the Old Testament and the Synoptic Gospels are to be viewed through the prisms of the Gospel of John through Revelation.

We have laid the foundation for contemplating the mysteries or secrets of God regarding the Church. Now the Mystery of the Faith draws our attention.

Look at the context of the verses below:

1 Timothy 3:2-10

2 A bishop then must be blameless, the husband of one wife, vigilant, sober, of good behaviour, given to hospitality, apt to teach;
3 Not given to wine, no striker, not greedy of filthy lucre; but patient, not a brawler, not covetous;
4 One that ruleth well his own house, having his children in subjection with all gravity;
5 (For if a man know not how to rule his own house, how shall he take care of the church of God?)
6 Not a novice, lest being lifted up with pride he fall into the condemnation of the devil.
7 Moreover he must have a good report of them which are without; lest he fall into reproach and the snare of the devil.
8 Likewise must the deacons be grave, not doubletongued, not given to much wine, not greedy of filthy lucre;
9 Holding the mystery of the faith in a pure conscience.
10 And let these also first be proved; then let them use the office of a deacon, being found blameless.

Paul's assignment from the Lord Jesus was to address the spiritual and practical qualifications of those who desired to serve a congregation as pastor (elder) and deacon. One of these qualifications is to: . . .*hold the mystery of the faith in a pure conscience.*

The first bit of information drawing our focus is the word *hold.* The idea is to hold in trust. For example, there was a time when the United States Government conducted its economic business based on a gold standard. That meant the people could count on the government not to print more money than the value of the physical gold held in trust at Kentucky's Fort Knox.

In this illustration, the government was holding in trust gold as support for the nation's economic system. In an analogous way, Paul is charging Timothy to verify that spiritual leaders use the Bible as their standard in teaching. In our case, the Bible is our Gold! Why? Because the Truth forms the very body of spiritual knowledge that is ours because of our unique relationship to God and His unique revelation to us. He has revealed Himself through: (1) the witness of creation (Romans 1:19, 20), (2) the conscience of man (Romans 2:15), and (3) the recorded witnesses like Moses, the prophets, and ultimately the Lord Jesus Christ Himself (2 Peter 1:21).

The church, by the end of the fourth century, had agreed upon the twenty-seven books we now have in The New Testament. The Holy Spirit had patiently gathered the twenty-seven writings into a completed library of sacred books to guide the Church in her earthly mission. The vast majority of Christians accept these divinely inspired letters as the very Word of God. The Holy Bible, compiled of sixty-six books making up both The Old and New Testaments, is the Christian's directive for faith and order for behavior.

This body of teaching became the Faith which was once delivered unto the saints (Jude 3). Generation after generation of believers have carefully guarded the Faith as a sacred trust before God. The Body of Faith as a whole and the Good News of grace in particular, is the first secret God has been pleased to show the church. The apostles themselves were not privileged to this complete body of information until after the instruction

Jesus had given to Paul. What the original twelve learned from Jesus had to be carefully merged with what Jesus taught Paul. Only then would the Truth become a complete body of information for all who followed.[40]

This same Pauline teaching, bestowed upon the early church, is now our Truth to hold in trust and pass to the next generation. We are to do this after the manner of Paul's instruction to Timothy where he wrote: *And the things that thou hast heard of me among many witnesses, the same commit thou to faithful men who shall be able to teach others also* (2 Timothy 2:2).

The biblical definition of faith is found in Hebrews 11:1. Consider it carefully:

> *Hebrews 11:1*
> *1 Now faith is the substance of things hoped for, the evidence of things not seen.*

God has given us reason to believe what He has promised. Why? Because His promises have authoritative certainty and a substance of reality. For example, God has promised those who believe His Word will inherit eternal life. God is the object of faith. We trust what He says in His Word. Even though we have not seen the Lord Jesus nor the prophets who prophesied about Him, we believe the evidence given us expresses the reality of His Truth.

We have numerous illustrations of faith exercised in the lives of biblical personalities. The most obvious ones are those recorded in Hebrews (Hebrews 11). We would do well to make these personalities a personal study. Doing so would

---

[40] Dr. Joe Duerr, who assisted in editing the manuscript, observed there is no contradiction in what Paul and the other apostles taught.

provide an understanding about the phenomenal grace given when faith is placed in what God has revealed.

We focus on several of these heroes as we strive to understand what faith means in the execution of daily life. A simple definition of faith is found in the phrases: *believing God* or *trusting God.*

The Example of Noah

In the times of Noah, the world was either in open rebellion against God or ignored God's revelation. It is difficult to comprehend how there could have been so few who worshiped the true God. Only Noah and his small family believed God and worshipped Him. The Lord came to Noah and instructed him to build an ark for safety (Genesis 6:5). The ark was to be a place of secure protection for the appointed creatures that would come into it. By this, these elected souls and creatures escape the judgment of the coming flood. God had grown intolerant of mankind's sin and determined to judge the world with a deluge of water that would encircle the earth and destroy every living creature outside the ark.

Contemplate the hindrances Noah had to endure in his trust and obedience. Here are some possibilities.

(1) It is likely he had to overcome a lie emanating from Satan that God would not really destroy the world. Such a suggestion would likely have caused Noah to doubt himself, whether God had actually instructed him to build an ark. Fits of unbelief would likely rise in his thoughts and war against the will of God he

had clearly understood. Why? Because God's instructions were precise!

(2) Man is a rational being and Noah likely would have had to wonder if the directions he had received from God were correct. It might not have made sense compared to all he had experienced. He had never seen rain, and he had never experienced a flood. Surely, he might have thought, God did not mean He was to build a boat. Because man's previous experience would indicate a boat would serve no practical purpose.

(3) Noah would have had to endure the mocking of his friends and neighbors who probably thought he had lost his senses. Noah would have had to overcome the social pressures caused by opinions of men based on every imaginable philosophy.

Noah deeply believed God had spoken to him. His experience was so real he obediently endured many years of social intolerance and abuse. He set his face like flint to complete his assignment. He did not turn aside; he did not abandon God's will. Being human, he had days of discouragement but he persevered through it all.

Some expositors have compared the likeness of Noah's ark to Christ. The two would be analogous in that the ark protected Noah and his family from the wrath of God displayed in the universal flood. Christ, as the Lamb of God, protects all sinners (who receive Him) from the judgment of God on sin displayed in Hell (John 3:16).

The Example of Abraham

Abram's father was Terah. He resided in Ur of Chaldea located in southern Mesopotamia. He had three sons Abram, Nahor, and Haran (Genesis 11:26, 1 Chronicles 1:26; Luke 3:34). Some believe Terah was a pagan idol maker and a practicing idolater. However in the providence of God, Terah decided to move to Canaan. He gathered his son Abram, Abram's wife Sarai, and Haran's son Lot, the rest of his family, and livestock, and set off to Canaan but stopped at the city of Haran. Haran lay in Paddan-aram a district in northwest Mesopotamia about 500 miles from Ur. The moon-god, Sin, was worshipped in both Haran and Ur. Some scholars believe a close relationship existed between the two cities despite the distance.

The extended stay in Haran ended after Terah's death. The Lord directed Abram to continue to Canaan. It appears that Abram was approximately 75 years old when his father died. Abram, Sarai and his nephew Lot along with the balance of his family and livestock began the arduous journey along the trade route to Canaan, referred to as the Fertile Crescent.

When Abram arrived in Canaan, the Lord appeared to him and promised him his children would inherit the land. This promise of God to Abram is the Abrahamic Covenant. God used this covenant to assure Abram that his people would have a central role in the redemptive plan for His people.

If you were to continue to read the rest of Abram's story, you would discover a man like most of us. He was a man of great faith, but he also exemplified signs of being a sinful man in need of God's mercy and grace. We see in Abram proof that God does not expect perfection from His people. But He does expect His people to depend on His perfect righteousness. Such dependence is revealed through daily obedience.

We know from the New Testament Abram looked to God for the fulfillment of all promises. We do not know how many details the Lord shared, but we do know that Abram believed God and it was accounted to him for righteousness (Galatians 3:6). Therefore, because he believed God, he was counted righteous by God. How could God count him righteous? Because, Abram placed his faith in what God revealed to him. We know there must be the shedding of blood for the forgiveness of sin (Hebrews 9:22). When God justified Abram, there was no shedding of blood! How, then, could God justify him?

God reveals the answer in a scene depicted in the following verse:

> *Revelation 13:8*
> *8 And all that dwell upon the earth shall worship him, whose names are not written in the book of life of the Lamb slain from the foundation of the world.*

Jesus reveals to John a prophecy about an end time event when a false spiritual leader will demand to be worshipped. Those who refuse to obey are those whose names are written in the Lamb's book of life. Notice the words ... *the Lamb slain from the foundation of the world.*

We conclude from the phrase that God justified Abram, because He applied to Abram the Lamb's blood shed before the foundation of the world. In man's history, the Lamb shed His blood, about AD 30, on a cross at Calvary. However, because of God's edict in eternity past, Christ's death for the sins of the world had become a reality before the creation of the world. Therefore, anyone who believes the witness of God is justified. Why? Because God applies (on their behalf) the blood from the substitutionary death of the Lamb.

We see from this instruction that every person, from any generation of mankind, who believes God's witness and worships God is received by Him because of the shed blood of His Son Jesus Christ. You find the basis for God's merciful forgiveness in the following words: . . . *the Lamb of God slain from the foundations of the world* (Revelation 13:8). You find a pertinent comment to this phrase in *The Whole Bible Commentary* by Jamison, Fausset and Brown.[41]

Those counted righteous by God have two facts in common: (1) they believe the testimony of God and (2) He justifies them because Jesus died for the sins of the world! There is no acceptance by God except for forgiveness through the blood sacrifice of His Son (Acts 4:12).

The Example of Paul

One is hard pressed to choose one over the many examples of faith from New Testament

---

[41]**Lamb slain from the foundation of the world**—The *Greek* order of words favors this translation. He was *slain* in the Father's eternal counsels: compare 1 Pe 1:19, 20, virtually parallel. The other way of connecting the words is, "Written from the foundation of the world in the book of life of the Lamb slain." So in Rev 17:8. The elect. The former is in the *Greek* more obvious and simple. "Whatsoever virtue was in the sacrifices, did operate through Messiah's death alone. As He was "the Lamb slain from the foundation of the world," so all atonements ever made were only effectual by His blood" [Bishop Pearson, *Exposition of the Creed*].

characters. However, the display of Saul's faith is likely the most dramatic and startling. It would be difficult to find anyone who was more culturally or religiously committed to Judaism than Saul. He sincerely believed he was a special servant of God, and yet being ignorant of who Jesus was, he persecuted the followers of Jesus (Acts 9).

Confronted on the road to Damascus by an unexplainable supernatural encounter, he was miraculously converted. In just moments after Jesus revealed Himself through the brilliance of light, Paul owns Him as Lord. His conversion was so complete he turned his back on all his previously held convictions about knowing God.

Saul threw himself upon the mercy of the very one who had been his avowed enemy. In that moment of destiny he surrendered all he had been to become all God had planned for him. How did he show his faith? He simply believed the witness of God. The circumstances of his conversion appear in Acts 9. The record states he believed the voice of the Son of God when he said . . . *I am Jesus whom you persecute* . . . (Acts 9:5). Immediately, upon hearing Jesus' voice, Saul directed his faith to God by placing trust in Jesus, whom he then recognized to be God in the flesh.

The encounter left him blind. He was led into Damascus and was without food or drink for three days. Ananias, instructed by the Holy Spirit, came to him and laid hands on him. It was as if scales fell from his eyes and he began immediately to preach Christ is the Messiah. When unbelieving Jews in Damascus heard of his conversion they sought to kill him. However, Paul escaped the plot. Christian brothers placed him in a basket and let him down by rope over the city wall.

He soon retreated into Arabia where he spent an extended period with Jesus. Paul was with Christ for three years (Galatians 1:15-20). During his training the Lord commissioned him to present the Gospel to Gentiles. He also received specific instructions about the Church and how she should function in the world.[42] When Jesus had finished Saul's training, He sent him first to the believers at Damascus and then on to Jerusalem to confer with the rest of the apostles.

In the days, months, and years that followed, Saul began to use his Roman name Paul. Why did he begin to utilize his Roman name? It was likely because he was witnessing in a Gentile world and being a Roman citizen afforded him certain advantages. Paul proved his faith by obedience to the call of God. He finally paid the ultimate human price by submitting to execution instead of denying what he knew to be true.

Exhortation

Our text says: *Holding the mystery of the faith in **a pure conscience*** (1 Timothy 3:9). Notice the highlighted phrase. The idea is one must not compromise one's integrity regarding convictions about God's revealed Truth as recorded in His Holy Word.

We can illustrate the principle by examining an event that occurred during the 1970's involving one of America's largest Protestant denominations. The rank and file membership believed in the supernatural claims of Scripture. For example, they believed in the virgin birth of Christ, the deity of

---

[42] Paul shared the instructions he received from Christ in his personal teaching, his epistles to the Churches, and his pastoral letters.

Christ, the physical resurrection of Christ from the dead, the Genesis account of creation and the history of mankind as depicted in the Bible.

Many of the denomination's universities and theological schools required teachers and tenured professors to sign an annual letter promising not to teach contrary to the denomination's doctrinal statement. They understood by signing the letter that immediate termination would follow their violation of the agreement.

As generation followed generation, some teachers began to believe contrary to the institution's doctrinal statement. These teachers did not seek employment elsewhere but chose to remain in their professorships and spout their dissenting dogma as *truth*. To continue such practice as a teacher in the denomination, they continued to sign the doctrinal statement with mental reservations. Perhaps they rationalized their understanding of Scripture was not out of step with the spirit of the original agreement. Therefore, they continued to sign the document with certain mental reservations. As the years passed some leading conservative pastors realized that young men and women were being graduated from their institutions of higher learning who did not hold to the doctrines in the denomination's statement of faith.

In 1967 I was pastoring a mid-sized rural church in SC. The pastor of a larger county seat church was discussing with me the doctrine of Christ's resurrection. He proudly informed me that Christ's resurrection was only spiritual in nature. I responded that the Bible declares Christ rose bodily from the dead. I then asked him where had learned that? In seminary, he responded and named one of the denominations premier institutions. That event illustrated for me the problem of not holding the faith with a pure conscience.

These young ministerial prodigies began echoing the subtle but destructive falsehoods espoused in the classroom. When confronted, many professors argued that they were within the bounds of academic license. They further argued the halls of learning required the inclusion of all competing ideas in order to maintain intellectual integrity. The conservatives countered by saying the introduction of competing philosophies was acceptable. However all teaching not supported by Scripture should be documented and presented as such by the professor. Any teacher not willing to follow such guidelines was expected to resign.

Many believed the treachery of false teaching was merely an attempt to bring the denomination into modern relevance. Despite motive, the said teachers were *not holding the faith with a pure conscience.* Such vows are accountable both to God and to the denomination from which they receive their financial support and whereto they owe their loyalty and authority to teach.

As the issue became public, the majority of these local universities broke off their alliances with the denomination and became independent entities. The theological institutions complied with the denomination's doctrinal position. Those teachers and administrative leaders unwilling to insure their doctrinal purity were asked to leave the employment of the denomination.

When the Lord asks us to believe, He asks us to embrace all He has declared. There is no room for mental reservations. The marvelous thing about God is His mercy. As long as you believe God's message is true, He will work with your doubts.

Remember the father of the demon possessed child? He said Lord I believe, help my unbelief (Mark 9:24).

To have mental reservations is to have an unstable mind. James, the brother of Jesus, said that such a person would not receive anything from the Lord. Read the account:

> *James 1:5-8*
> *5 If any of you lack wisdom, let him ask of God, that giveth to all men liberally, and upbraideth not; and it shall be given him.*
> *6 But let him ask in faith, nothing wavering. For he that wavereth is like a wave of the sea driven with the wind and tossed.*
> *7 For let not that man think that he shall receive any thing of the Lord.*
> *8 A double minded man is unstable in all his ways.*

Why doesn't God reward the double minded man? Because God does not reward unbelief. To not believe God is unbelief and the pinnacle of rebellion. Unbelief is a grievous insult to the integrity of God. God is patient with a person who exercises his will to obey but may wrestle with the purpose or even the rationale for it. Such rationale is never justifiable, but it is certainly human and God knows our weaknesses and will forgive the sin of unbelief when genuinely confessed.

Believers struggle against the world, the flesh, and the devil. Each of us must resolve to be faithful to God's charge. We must hold the faith of God's Truth with a pure conscience. A pretentious faith will not work. God will not play games with us; He will not be fooled by our pretense. We must place our faith in the testimony of God's Word and resolve, by His grace, to obey it.

You and I are privileged to hold the teachings (embodied in the Bible) in trust. We hold them for the next generation. We must continue in the spirit of 2 Timothy 2:2, where he teaches us to share our faith with another, that he in turn may share with other faithful believers.

The Truth entrusted to us is precious and essential for the glory of God and the salvation of mankind. Every generation of believers, every church, every Christian institution must understand the gravity of the trust God has placed in us to keep the standard of His Truth measured by the inerrant Word of God.

From my vantage point, it appears Christians in America have failed miserably in holding God's Word in trust. For example, the early academic institutions of higher learning in America failed their charge from God to pass on the faithful message of God's Word. Institutions like Yale, Harvard and Brown were once stalwarts for Bible Truth. As the so-called *age of enlightenment* impacted America these great institutions, founded to train ministers for the propagation of the Gospel, began to drift away from their spiritual moorings. Eventually, their standard for life became the discoveries of secular science. Rather than interpret scientific discoveries by God's revealed Truth, they chose to judge God's Word in light of their secular and naturalistic discoveries. Thus, most academies in America and Europe have abandoned faith in the Bible as a sure Word from God.

The Satanic lie has extended from Eden's garden to this very day. Lying is one of Satan's most effective ploys as he seeks to derail God's purpose of restoring His creation to its former glory. We may be sure God is faithful to preserve in every generation a remnant who will survive and will hold His Truth in trust to the praise of His name.

Questions for Discussion

1. Describe the Mystery of the Faith.

2. What is faith as used in revealing the mystery?

3. What does it mean to hold in trust?

4. In the context of 1 Timothy 3:9, what does it mean to hold the faith in a pure conscience?

Chapter 4

The Mystery Of
Union With Christ
(The Church)

The secret of Christ's union with his people is all about the union of the Church set forth as His Body and His Bride.

When Paul received his instructions from the Lord Jesus, the Church had been a secret hidden in the heart of God before the world began. God held the secret until He revealed it through His Son; first He alluded to it during His ministry in Galilee and Judea, and then He fully shared it with Paul in His post resurrection ministry in Arabia.

Paul now shares these dynamic teachings in his epistles.

Explanation

Christian mystics have written numerous books and articles about the unique union believers have with their Savior. When I use the term *Christian mystic* I mean to reference one who emphasizes the spiritual aspects of faith and seeks to practice an awareness of the presence of God in daily life through prayer and biblical meditation.[43]

The Church was not fully revealed in the Old Testament or in the Gospels. It was alluded to by the Lord on several occasions but never explained. It was not fully revealed until the Lord taught Paul in Arabia. Only then did the Church develop as an entity. The fact that Christ alluded to it in the Gospels confirms for us that the Church was not an afterthought or a back-up plan for completing His plan for the ages. It was in the plan of God before the world's creation.

The fact that Christ's union with the Church had not been earlier shown and was a mysterious concept, made Paul's task even more difficult. Why? Because he was dealing with people whose minds were predisposed to Judaism. He had to overcome the suspicion that he was a Jewish spy sent to discover who the Christian leaders were. After gaining their confidence through the witness of Barnabas, Paul had the responsibility and the amazing privilege of explaining the supernatural reality of believers being in union with Christ.

---

[43] Some examples of Christian mystics are: George Mueller, Brother Lawrence, A. W. Tozer, Andrew Murray, Oswald Chambers, Bertha Smith, etc.

Exposition

We begin by examining Ephesians 5:17-33.

The passage is divided into four sections to assist us in understanding its emphasis. Carefully read the first section.

Ephesians 5:17-21
17 Wherefore be ye not unwise, but understanding what the will of the Lord is.
18 And be not drunk with wine, wherein is excess; but be filled with the Spirit;
19 Speaking to yourselves in psalms and hymns and spiritual songs, singing and making melody in your heart to the Lord;
20 Giving thanks always for all things unto God and the Father in the name of our Lord Jesus Christ;
21 Submitting yourselves one to another in the fear of God.

The Lord here presents us with the second and perhaps the most foundational of the secrets revealed to Paul. He explains the secret here and mentions it in many of his Epistles.[44] The above passage is not primarily about wives submitting to their husbands. The word *submit* is here depicted as the ultimate expression of worship. Why? Because, Paul uses the rapturous relationship of a groom and his bride to express the spiritual relationship believers have with Christ. Note phrases like: . . .*be filled with the Spirit,* . . .

---

[44] The union of Christ and the Church are mentioned also in Romans 12:5, 1 Corinthians 12:12, and Ephesians 1:22, 23.

Speaking to yourselves in . . . songs, singing and making melody in your heart.

The above words express the natural feelings of a new bride for her groom and the groom for his bride. Understand clearly, I am not suggesting that we reduce our spiritual worship of Christ to lustful feelings of the flesh. However I see Paul using the analogy to invoke spiritual worship from our hearts to Christ, who is our spiritual Groom. He writes about this union as supernatural in nature and is the basis of all his spiritual instructions.

Look with me at the second section contained in verses 22-24:

> *22 Wives, submit yourselves unto your own husbands, as unto the Lord.*
> *23 For the husband is the head of the wife, even as Christ is the head of the church: and he is the saviour of the body.*
> *24 Therefore as the church is subject unto Christ, so let the wives be to their own husbands in every thing.*

We want to focus here on the relationship of the Church to Christ. We may ask: *What is Christ to us?* He is not only our *Savior, He is* our *Head.* What is to be our response to Him? Our response is to submit to Him in love and adoration, knowing He loves us and He gave Himself for us.

In our submission we become His instruments of grace in our world bearing a faithful testimony to the faith entrusted to us. He watches over us, guides us, teaches us, comforts us, and promises never to leave us. He does all this and more through God the Holy Spirit.

Now focus on the third section in verses 25-29:

25 Husbands, love your wives, even as Christ also loved the church, and gave himself for it;
26 That he might sanctify and cleanse it with the washing of water by the word,
27 That he might present it to himself a glorious church, not having spot, or wrinkle, or any such thing; but that it should be holy and without blemish.
28 So ought men to love their wives as their own bodies. He that loveth his wife loveth himself.
29 For no man ever yet hated his own flesh; but nourisheth and cherisheth it, even as the Lord the church:

In these verses Paul informs us about (1) what Christ is doing for the Church, (2) how He presents the Church to Himself, and (3) what He continually does for the Church.

What is He doing for His Bride (the Church)?

In verses twenty-five and twenty-six, we see the members of the Church being sanctified by the Holy Spirit at this very moment. He continues to do the same for others as more are added to the Church. He sanctifies or sets us aside by continually cleansing us through our study of the Bible. It is from the Bible that we come to understand the Truths of God. As we read and meditate on the Word, the Holy Spirit illuminates it. In doing so, He makes clear its meaning and application to our lives.

Our sanctification is experienced by those around us as we obey the Holy Spirit's prompting. In obeying Him, we show the fruit of the Spirit working in us and flowing out of our lives into the lives of others. Our actions like kindness, mercy, goodness, etc., show the Holy Spirit working in us (Galatians 5:22, 23).

How does He present Himself to the Church?

In verses twenty-seven and twenty-eight we observe that He is presenting the Church as pure, without spot or blemish. He does this by applying to us His own purity and righteousness. When we believe in Christ, the Holy Spirit positions us spiritually in heaven with the risen Christ (Ephesians 2:6). Spiritually we take on the purity we will actually experience in our glorified state.

What does He continue to do for the Church?

In verse twenty-nine the Holy Spirit reminds us that believers are continually being nourished and cherished. What does that mean? It means that as we meditate on God's Truth, His Spirit cherishes and nourishes us with a heightened awareness of both the meaning of Scripture and His presence in our daily life. As we cherish our own family members, so God cherishes us because we are in Christ.

Let us now look at the final section, verses thirty through thirty-three.

30 For we are members of his body, of his flesh, and of his bones.
31 For this cause shall a man leave his father and mother, and shall be joined unto his wife, and they two shall be one flesh.
32 This is a great mystery: but I speak concerning Christ and the church.
33 Nevertheless let every one of you in particular so love his wife even as himself;

and the wife see that she reverence her husband.

This section of the passage answers the question: *What are we to do as believers?*

We find In verse thirty we should recognize our relationship to Christ as members of His body. As in marriage, a husband and his wife are joined; in Christ we are joined to Him as His bride.

Paul informs us in verse thirty-two that the primary purpose of the passage is to illustrate the supernatural union and spiritual experience that exists between Christ and His Church. This mystical or supernatural union is the revealed mystery or secret that had been kept in the heart of God until this time. The use of the word *mystical* stresses the supernatural nature of its reality. Look more closely at how Paul explains this phenomenon by using the union of marriage between a man and a woman as an illustration.

Exhortation

We first look at his instructions leading into the analogy. In verses seventeen through twenty-one he speaks of (1) the need for spiritual wisdom, (2) being filled with the Spirit, (3) worshipping God from the heart, (4) offering thanksgiving in the Savior's name, and (5) submitting to one-another in reverencing God. The operative idea is found in the word *submitting*.

Paul introduces these five elements to describe the reality of the mystery. Notice one may not experience the reality of this spiritual union unless all five elements are operational. For example, it appears they flow one into the other. It all begins with spiritual wisdom which is a grace gift from the Lord. Having spiritual wisdom, one may then be filled with the Holy Spirit and spiritual worship will then proceed from the heart.[45] Spiritual worship manifests itself in prayerful thanksgiving and an attitude of submission to spiritual authority.

When all five aspects, listed by Paul, in this Ephesian passage are operational, then one may be assured a union with Christ is fully functional. Only willful or deliberate sin will disrupt the union. However, be assured, repentance and confession will result in forgiveness and restoration of the union (1 John 1:8, 9).

Christian submission is all about seeing others spiritually succeed. The ultimate example of submission is Christ in the garden of Gethsemane when He cried out . . . *not my will but thine be done* (Luke 22:42). The Savior, who has equal authority with the Father, submitted Himself to the will of the Father so the Father's plan for restoring all creation would bring the Father glory (John 17:1). The Son does not seek His own glory, only the glory of the Father, while the Spirit seeks the glory of the Son (John 17:4; Matthew 3:16).

It is intriguing that our Lord should use the analogy of marriage to explain the mystery of the Christian's union with Christ. The analogy relates to the most intimate of human relationships. He alludes to the indescribable intimacy and physical union experienced by a man and woman in marriage as a parallel to the spiritual union experienced by the Christian when he is born again (John 3:3). The new birth occurs when the sinner

---

[45]Natural wisdom is our ability to properly use knowledge gained through experience. Spiritual wisdom is a supernatural discernment from God that enables us to apply biblical principles to daily activity.

believes God's witness and declares his faith in Christ. The Father grants saving grace as the sinner submits to Christ as Lord and Savior (John 3:16; Romans 10:9, 10).

Putting another's will before your own is an unnatural act for sinful man (Romans 3:23). While one without God may submit his will to another, generally he only does so if he in someway benefits. The Savior's acts of selflessness are contrary to sinners like us. The true believer, acting out of spiritual maturity, will show the same kinds of selflessness demonstrated by Jesus because of his personal union with Christ.

The mystery of Christ's union with His people is a spiritual reality existing on three levels: personal, corporate, and universal.

We explain our first level as having a personal experience with Christ, without which there can be no union. But, where a union exists, it links to two other levels. These are spiritual levels and include both the physical and invisible. We explain the physical level by referencing the public gathering of the local congregation called a Church.

Drawn to one another because of our union with Christ, we begin to take on the spiritual characteristics of His mind or the way He thinks. His Spirit permeates our spirit as we submit to His instruction.

He grants us, as Christians, spiritual gifts so that we may effectively serve one another (Romans 12; I Corinthians 12-14). These gifts are supernatural enablements. We see them expressed in spiritual and practical service. Believers are the various members of one body where all members serve one another. Most members will function uniquely to their particular gifts, but all will exercise or use their gifts to promote the spiritual success of others for the cause and glory of Christ.

A Christian church is a group of baptized believers who in Christ's name meet regularly to worship God and to study His Word (the Holy Bible). They are a people who were spiritually baptized into Christ by the Holy Spirit and have one common purpose: the worship of God through His Son Jesus Christ. These physical gatherings or assemblies are visible as they gather in various communities. These gatherings normally take place in a meeting hall. Some call the meeting places churches, temples, or houses of God.

Paul has not depicted *church* as an institution or even a denomination of churches. There is only one Church, and it is made up of individual Christians, assembling with one another in different locations to worship the one true God through Jesus Christ the Son of God. Therefore, there is no perfect Church or denomination. Why? Because, all people who believe in and are committed to Jesus Christ are Christians and members of His body (the Church). His body is likely found in every denomination. The fact that we Christians divide ourselves along doctrinal lines is both a blessing and a curse. It is a blessing because it should minimize arguments over our teaching. But, it is also a curse because our division grieves our Lord.

Because of our denominational differences, we should work at minimizing disagreement between us. How? We can start by recognizing (without respect to denomination) that all who trust the finished work of Christ, are brothers and sisters in the same faith. Our loyalty must be to Christ first, and then to our particular denomination.

There is another sense in which the church is both invisible and universal. In her universal and invisible sense, she comprises every person who has ever received Christ as Lord from every generation since the beginning of Christ's earthly ministry. They are members of His body called the *Bride of Christ*. The universal Church will have her initial gathering when Christ calls her to meet Him in the air at the sound of the trumpet. Paul records this event in 1 Thessalonians 4:13-18. We will discuss this passage in greater detail when we contemplate *The Mystery of the Rapture*.

Questions for Discussion

1. Define the term *The Bride of Christ.*

2. Describe the human experience that most closely illustrates the union of Christ with His people called the *Church.*

3. List the five elements (suggested by the author) in Ephesians 5:17-33 that allow us to understand what a union with Christ looks like in daily experience.

4. When is a union with Christ a spiritual reality?

Chapter 5

The Mystery Of Christ's Indwelling

In the Old Covenant, we observe God coming upon men with anointing power to accomplish His will. He came upon Moses and used him to lead Israel out of Egyptian bondage. He empowered David to slay Goliath. He came upon Elijah when he prayed and called down fire from heaven and destroyed the prophets of Baal. He empowered a repentant Samson and in his blindness he pulled down the pillars and the enemies of God were destroyed in the rubble. The Old Testament is replete with examples of how God has come upon His people to accomplish His purpose in gaining victory over sin and the enemies of righteousness.

Now a new day dawns for a new people!

In the New Covenant, Jesus reveals to Paul a new and more intimate relationship to further the Father's purposes. Paul writes about it in his epistle to the Colossians.[46]

Explanation

God establishes a new and intimate relationship with those whom He is calling out as His servants, and disciples of His Son Jesus. These believers have a new nature residing in them.

Paul introduces the concept to the Colossians because the Holy Spirit determined it was time to explain a reality never experienced by man before. Abraham, Moses, the prophets, David, Solomon and even the apostles had never known this spiritual reality (prior to Acts 2) that gives the servant of God an extraordinary witness that God is with him. (The only possible exception I know of is in John 20:21 when the resurrected Jesus breathed on them and the apostles received the Holy Spirit.) How does this mystery unfold in the Christian's life?

The two passages under consideration relate to two vastly different church situations. The first is the Galatia church, probably comprised of members from several closely related villages in Galatia where Paul had ministered on two previous occasions. However, the Colossians' church was different because Paul had never visited there. They had likely heard the Gospel through Epaphras. He

---

[46] As seen in Part II, chapter 3, the new entity introduced by God is the Church. God's focus on the Church does not diminish His love or commitment to Israel. A more literal interpretation of Scripture leads us to believe we are now in a parenthesis of time in which God is focusing His attention on the Gentiles. When the Church is complete Israel will once again become the focus of His attention (Revelation 12:7-17).

was a disciple of Paul mentioned in both the letter to the church at Colossae and the one to Philemon.

While Paul had different reasons for writing the two churches, there was a shared central truth. Each needed to know the peace of God and freedom from the bondage of sin and how to deal with temptation. Knowing the presence of peace and how to overcome temptations are provided in the secret Paul learned from the Lord Jesus.

(handwritten margin note: Current Today!)

Exposition

We examine the following passages for an answer: Colossians 1:21-29 and Galatians 2:20; 5:16-26. Read carefully the Colossians passage:

> *Colossians 1:21-29*
> *21 And you, that were sometime alienated and enemies in your mind by wicked works, yet now hath he reconciled*
> *22 In the body of his flesh through death, to present you holy and unblameable and unreproveable in his sight:*
> *23 If ye continue in the faith grounded and settled, and be not moved away from the hope of the gospel, which ye have heard, and which was preached to every creature which is under heaven; whereof I Paul am made a minister;*
> *24 Who now rejoice in my sufferings for you, and fill up that which is behind of the afflictions of Christ in my flesh for his body's sake, which is the church:*
> *25 Whereof I am made a minister, according to the dispensation of God which is given to me for you, to fulfil the word of God;*
> *26 Even the mystery which hath been hid from ages and from generations, but now is made*

manifest to his saints:
27 To whom God would make known what is
the riches of the glory of this mystery among
the Gentiles; which is Christ in you, the hope
of glory:
28 Whom we preach, warning every man, and
teaching every man in all wisdom; that we
may present every man perfect in Christ
Jesus:
29 Whereunto I also labour, striving according
to his working, which worketh in me mightily.

In verses twenty-one through twenty-three, Paul reminds his readers that all sinners are alienated from God. However, he hastens to also say everyone who receives Christ as Savior is at one with God. Oneness with God is based on Christ's sacrificial and substitutionary death. He died so believers would not have to experience spiritual death or separation from God forever.[47]

However, notice in verse twenty-three the use of the *if* clause: *If ye continue in the faith grounded and settled,. . ..* The grammar is constructed so that we are reminded of man's responsibility to continue exercising *faith* in all that God has said for the balance of one's life.

Once you believe God's message of hope, the Holy Spirit supernaturally baptizes you into the *body of Christ*. As you continue to walk in obedience, He continually confirms your faith.

---

[47] Physical death comes upon all Adam's descendants because his sin made his offspring sinners by nature. Having a sin nature means we are drawn to sin like metal is drawn to a magnet. Because the physical body is corrupted by sin the Scripture says flesh and blood cannot inherit the kingdom of God (1 Corinthians 15:50). Therefore, death comes upon all earth dwellers as sons of Adam. However, the second death is separation from God forever in torment (Revelation). The second death is reserved for those who reject Christ.

Angels in the spiritual realm rejoice and celebrate when sinners come to Christ and become part of *His body*. As indicated in the last chapter, the *body of Christ* is serving Him in the physical world through the empowerment of spiritual gifts (Romans 12:6-8; 1 Corinthians 12:1-11; Ephesians 4:7-12).

Next, focus on a phrase in verse twenty seven. This phrase contains the heart and soul of the secret: *Christ in you, the hope of glory*. As we search for understanding, God's Word is our only reference for accurate information.

In searching the Word it is natural to ask questions. But make sure you are not leaning on your own reasoning for understanding (Psalm 3:5). We are prone to reinterpret the Word to fit our own cultural bias. It is best to read the Word for what it clearly says. Then, let Scripture interpret Scripture. Draw your conclusions from what the Word says, not what you think or feel. Nor should you take the opinions of others when not based on the Word. Remember, Satan is a deceiver, a liar, and often comes to us as an *angel of light*. He often works through all levels of large and small organizations, groups having various interests, individuals, and sometimes misguided Christians who do not rely on the Word for their guidance.

In the following paragraphs are some questions we might ask to aid us in our search for Truth.

How do you know Christ is in you?

The answer is directly related to how you respond to God's promises. For example, because you trusted God's promise, you took action on the basis of His promise. Therefore, because you took action based on faith that what He told you is true, God counted you justified on the basis of Christ's substitutionary death on your behalf. You are now embraced by Him as He embraced Abraham when he believed God (Hebrews 11:8-11).

Therefore you know by faith you are in Christ and Christ is in you (John 14:20). However, let me remind you, it is not a cafeteria style list of promises from which you may pick and choose the most appealing ones. You must choose Him based on what He says about Himself; you must will to obey all He says. You may not always succeed, but it should be your will to do so.

If you will come to Him, He will receive you and come into your life.

What does it mean to have Jesus in you?

Having Christ in you means the Spirit of Christ actually lives in your spirit. No one can explain how this reality takes place. We can only share what we are taught in the Scripture. From our Scriptural authority, we know Christ's indwelling is a supernatural act granted by the Holy Spirit the moment you surrender your life to Christ. It may not seem real to you at first; however I can assure you His presence is real, even if it does not seem so at this stage in your Christian development. We must learn not to trust feelings as a test of Truth.

As you grow spiritually, an awareness of His presence will become more apparent. Even the most mature Christians have some difficulty verbalizing their experience of Christ's indwelling. However, they have no difficulty witnessing to the reality of His presence.

We have an example in Brother Lawrence, a French monk, who learned how to live daily with an awareness of God's presence. After his death, a fellow priest collected his writings and published them under the title *The Practice of the Presence of God.* [48] In his writings he describes the principles and maxims that the Lord gave him for daily living. Through the diligent application of these maxims, he daily walked with the Lord and was conscious of His presence continually and blessed those around him.

How can we cooperate with Christ?

To answer this question about the Christian life, we need to consider the following:

Ephesians 1:3-6
3 Blessed be the God and Father of our Lord Jesus Christ, who hath blessed us with all spiritual blessings in heavenly places in Christ:
4 According as he hath chosen us in him before the foundation of the world, that we should be holy and without blame before him in love:
5 Having predestinated us unto the adoption of children by Jesus Christ to himself, according to the good pleasure of his will,
6 To the praise of the glory of his grace, wherein he hath made us accepted in the beloved.

In this passage Paul tells us what the believer's position is in Christ. He witnesses that Christians

---

[48] The book is in public domain but I suppose because it is translated from French each translation is a new copy-write. It is widely available in both print an ebook format.

have an eternal identification with the living Savior. He says that before God created the world and its related planets, galaxies and universes, He set in place a flawless plan whereby the entirety of His people (who believe Him) will be redeemed from sin and made holy (Ephesians 1:3-6). We can cooperate with Christ by being obedient to the leading of the Holy Spirit. When we are obedient in following Him we will do things that bring glory to His name and joy to His heart.

What does the phrase . . . *Christ in you the hope of glory* . . . mean?

Most commentators express an opinion favoring a view from the believer's perspective. Therefore, it would mean *Christ in you* is your hope for glory or heaven. However, could it not also be viewed from God's perspective? If so, it would mean *Christ in you* is heaven's hope. And what is hoped for? Christ in you is God's hope for the restoration of His glory and your blessing.[49] Therefore, God is honored and the believer receives inheritance with Christ.

Exhortation

Paul wrote that the redeemed will be known by their love and their behavior. Their lifestyle will reveal their heart motive as servants of Christ. What does holy and righteous behavior look like? It is described in the following verses.

Galatians 5:16-26
16 I say then, Walk in the Spirit, and ye shall

---

[49] God would be dependent upon Christ in believers only because it is the means through which He declared He would reclaim His Trinitarian glory. It does not mean that He is dependent upon the faithfulness of man; it means He is dependent on His Spirit in man (Hebrews 13:20, 21).

not fulfil the lust of the flesh.
17 For the flesh lusteth against the Spirit, and
the Spirit against the flesh: and these are
contrary the one to the other: so that ye cannot
do the things that ye would.

18 But if ye be led of the Spirit, ye are not
under the law.
19 Now the works of the flesh are manifest,
which are these; Adultery, fornication,
uncleanness, lasciviousness,
20 Idolatry, witchcraft, hatred, variance,
emulations, wrath, strife, seditions, heresies,
21 Envyings, murders, drunkenness,
revellings, and such like: of the which I tell you
before, as I have also told you in time past,
that they which do such things shall not
inherit the kingdom of God.
22 But the fruit of the Spirit is love, joy, peace,
longsuffering, gentleness, goodness, faith,
23 Meekness, temperance: against such there
is no law.
24 And they that are Christ's have crucified
the flesh with the affections and lusts.
25 If we live in the Spirit, let us also walk in
the Spirit.
26 Let us not be desirous of vain glory,
provoking one another, envying one another.

Paul has described the difference between the Spirit controlled man (verses 22, 23) and the man controlled by his fleshly desires and unnatural appetites (verses 19-21).

The *old man* is controlled by his fleshly desires and often driven to acquire control or power. Paul lists seventeen characteristics that mirror the behavior of a person controlled by his own desires. God's Word Translation gives us this list: *illicit sex, perversion, promiscuity, idolatry, drug use, hatred, rivalry, jealousy, angry outbursts, selfish ambition, conflict, factions, envy, drunkenness, wild partying, and things like that.*[50]

A person controlled by any one of these fleshly characteristics or motivations is a person driven by his natural condition and is either separated from God or is a believer in a backslidden condition and out of fellowship with God. Therefore, it is not enough to measure behavior alone, consideration must also be given to motive. While it is not the responsibility of one to judge another, we must be discerning of one another's actions and the spirit in which those actions are implemented (Galatians 6:1,2; I John 4:1) .

A person controlled by the Spirit produces the fruit of the Spirit. Spiritual fruit does not come because of fleshly energy, but by spiritual energy given by the Holy Spirit as one abides in Christ (John 15). As abiding believers, we are exhorted by Paul to present our body a living sacrifice (Romans 12:1).

This means you rise from your sleep reporting for duty. It is a continuous commitment to His will. You recognize you are an ambassador for Christ. You are His representative at home, at school, in your work place, in your clubs, and in your personal relationships. The Holy Spirit works in you and through you to accomplish God's goals right where you are. Consider yourself planted by the Master Gardener who is working in you as you grow (Phillipians 2:13).

---

[50] *GOD'S WORD Translation* (Grand Rapids: Baker Publishing Group, 1995), Ga 5:19–21.

You may be God's only representative where He has placed you. But you are only an effective ambassador when you obey Him. Your obedience becomes the standard by which you measure yourself and by which you will be known. Your faithfulness to and love for God will mark you as His.

Our righteous behavior is not the work of our *old man*, but the Holy Spirit, who is at work through the *new man.* Why? Because, *the old man* is crucified with Christ and is therefore dead to God. Because Christ died for your sins, God counts your *old man* dead. The *old man* cannot please God nor do anything to merit God's pleasure. Why? Because he is the body of sin and is therefore corrupt. However, your *new man* is alive because he is identified with Christ and His resurrection. You live because Christ lives! Believers are now empowered by Christ's indwelling Spirit. The *new man* is now in the family of God and made a joint heir with Jesus. Look at what Romans 8:17 says: *And if children, then heirs; heirs of God, and joint-heirs with Christ; if so be that we suffer with him, that we may be also glorified together.*

Jesus does not teach us to be physically passive. He teaches us to rest, spiritually, in Him as we go about the affairs of physical life. As we exert physical effort to accomplish God's goals, the Holy Spirit will produce His fruit in us and provide the necessary energy to accomplish His purposes (John 15:7, 8).

God provides with the Holy Spirit who guides, instructs, comforts, and convicts the believer. The Christian life is a series of experiences directed by God to assure the believer arrives at the desired destination of completeness in Christ (Romans 8:28, 29; Hebrews 13:20, 21).

The believer responds to the Holy Spirit's leadership:

1. He responds by counting himself in the heavens with Christ (Ephesians 1:20; Romans 8:39). (This means that at this very moment believers are in the very heart of Christ as He sits at the Father's right hand of authority and nothing can separate us from the love of God. Since He is there we are there also in a spiritual sense. It is our spiritual position.)

2. He responds by counting himself free from the judgment of the Law (Romans 8:1; Romans 2:14,15). (Believers are free, not because they live a clean or good life, but because Jesus died for their sins and has forgiven them. By contrast, man without Christ is guilty of sin because he violates the Law of God and he must bear the weight of his sin. Without Christ he has no acceptable sacrifice for his sin. Though one is free from the judgment of the Law, he is not free from the moral truths taught in the Law. Why? Because the Law reflects the character of God and therefore we will reflect His character in the way we live.)

3. He responds by counting himself dead to the condemning power of sin (Romans 6:6; 11). (When faced with temptation, Christians have an ally in their hearts in the person of the Holy Spirit who enables them to count themselves in Christ and therefore dead to sin. It does not mean they are not tempted in the flesh, it means they deny the flesh by calling on the power of God residing in them.)

4. He responds by counting himself holy or complete in Christ (James 1:4). (The Scriptures implore Christians to be holy in their behavior. This is only possible when Christ provides us with His own righteousness. This He has done. Though we may continue to falter and fail many tests and trials, our position is ever secure in Christ.)

5. He responds by counting himself resting in Christ (the vine) to provide him with the spiritual energy or life to live abundantly to God's glory (John 15:5).

6. He responds by counting himself as having God's enabling presence every moment of every day. (This includes life's blessings as well as the dark times. When trials and temptations come God can be depended on to provide strength and grace to face it or provide us a way to escape (Hebrews 13:5; 1 Corinthians 10:13).

The above is not an exhaustive list of the benefits that believers possess, but knowing and understanding these can bring bounding joy and purpose to the Christian's life.

Questions for Discussion

1. Define the term *The Church of Jesus Christ.*

2. Describe the human experience that most closely illustrates the indwelling of Christ in His people called the *Church.*

3. List the six ways (suggested by the author) the believer shows he is following the leadership of the Holy Spirit.

4. When is is the indwelling of Christ a spiritual reality?

Chapter 6

The Mystery Of Israel's Blindness

The descendants of Abraham were chosen of God to be His witness to the nations of the world. Abraham's offspring became known as *Israel,* named after one of Abraham's grandsons. God did not choose them because they were worthy, brilliant, industrious, or any reason that impresses man. God chose Israel because it pleased Him and for no other reason. He established a covenant with them that promised earthly rewards, such as making them a large nation of people. God also promised they would be a blessing to the nations of the world (Genesis 17:5-11).

Israel, as a nation, has had many periods of faithfulness to God and many seasons of unbelief and idol worship. In each of these negative seasons of unbelief and unfaithfulness, God has shown His longsuffering and patience. Even when God judged their sins, He lovingly drew them back to Himself.

Through the centuries our faithful Lord has maintained His witness through leaders like Abraham, Issac, Jacob, Moses, and Joshua. He also gave them prophets like Isaiah, Jeremiah, Ezekiel, Jonah, and Malachi. As judgment for their sins He would sometimes allow their enemies to overcome them and take them into exile, making them slaves in other lands.

At the right time, the Lord would allow them to return to their land and rebuild Jerusalem. After the rebuilding, there have been numerous conquerers who have overtaken them, mutilated them, and desecrated the temple. It was not until approximately 165 BC that temple worship was re-established during the Maccabean period.

After the prophet Malachi, there was a long period of silence with no word from God. For approximately 400 years, God withheld His presence from idolatrous Israel. Even their worship of the Lord had become heretical because they intermingled their erroneous traditions with the pure Word of God.

It appears the deafening silence was a judgment on Israel's unbelief and spiritual idolatry. Again, God was not taken by surprise. He used their unbelief to open the door to invite the Gentile nations to receive His message. God's plan for the ages is to restore His creation to a sinless and glorious state. His plan is on schedule!

The silence was finally penetrated by an obscure but miraculous birth. God sent a final Prophet in the person of His Son Jesus Christ. He was sent to His own people but they did not receive Him because they were spiritually blind (John 1:11).

Explanation

To understand this mystery of Israel's blindness or unbelief, we must look to the revelation of God's Word. In the Scriptures we find that even during periods of lawlessness and idolatry, God has had his remnant.

For example, look at the word of the prophet Isaiah.

> *Isaiah 10:20-22*
> *20 And it shall come to pass in that day,*
> *That the remnant of Israel, And such as are*
> *escaped of the house of Jacob, Shall no more*
> *again stay upon him that smote them; But*
> *shall stay upon the Lord, The Holy One of*
> *Israel, in truth.*
> *21 The remnant shall return, even the remnant*
> *of Jacob, Unto the mighty God.*
> *22 For though thy people Israel be as the sand*
> *of the sea, Yet a remnant of them shall return:*
> *The consumption decreed shall overflow with*
> *righteousness.*

Notice the underlined phrases that include the word *remnant*. In every generation, God has reserved unto Himself a remnant according to His purpose.

Another example is Elijah. You may recall Elijah's depression after having conquered the prophets of Baal. He thought himself the only one left in all the land who faithfully served God. But God met Elijah in his depression, and reminded him that He had 7000 who had not bowed the knee to Baal (1 Kings 19:18).

Because Israel was spiritually fickle, we assume God spiritually blinded all except a remnant during the presentation of His Son as the appointed Messiah. It is He, the sacrificial Lamb, who takes away the sins of the world.

Exposition

There is a central passage we must examine because it is only one of two in which Paul specifically mentions this particular mystery. It is the mystery of Israel's blindness or hardened hearts.

> *Romans 11:25-30*
> *25 For I would not, brethren, that ye should be ignorant of this mystery, lest ye should be wise in your own conceits; that blindness in part is happened to Israel, until the fulness of the Gentiles be come in.*
> *26 And so all Israel shall be saved: as it is written, There shall come out of Sion the Deliverer, and shall turn away ungodliness from Jacob:*
> *27 For this is my covenant unto them, when I shall take away their sins.*
> *28 As concerning the gospel, they are enemies for your sakes: but as touching the election, they are beloved for the fathers' sakes.*
> *29 For the gifts and calling of God are without repentance.*
> *30 For as ye in times past have not believed God, yet have now obtained mercy through their unbelief:*

Contextually, Paul has already declared in chapters 1-3 of Romans that all men, both Jew and Gentile, are worthy of rejection and God's judgment. However, in His mercy God provided acceptance for sinners through His Son, the substitute sacrifice for the sins of the world (John 3:16).

In Romans 4, Paul presents the argument that Abraham was accepted by God purely based on believing God (Romans 4:3). He continued in his argument that the works of the Law did not merit him in his relationship with God. Man's only hope for acceptance with God is grace, and it may only be obtained through faith in God's message.

In Romans 5-8 he writes of justification before God and sanctification in and by God. He writes about personal conflict with his *old man* and the *new man*. The indwelling law of righteousness that is the presence of the Holy Spirit, is opposing the *old man, the flesh*. He closes the section by showing that the Christian's victory is following the indwelling Spirit of the resurrected Christ.

Now in chapters 9-11 Paul turned his attention to Israel's unbelief. It is not that they did not believe in God; the problem was their interpretation of the Scriptures revealing God. They had preconceived notions about the Messiah that were erroneous. Their thoughts about how He would come, and how He would deal with the nations of the world, would not allow them to accept Jesus. They could not believe God would humble Himself to dwell in human flesh. It was beyond their capacity to believe the Messiah would be born in a manger, grow up in an average home, be crucified as a criminal and become the Lamb of God for the sins of the world.

Paul was greatly concerned for Israel's salvation and repeatedly appealed to them from the Scriptures about Christ. He even went so far as to declare his heart's desire that they might be saved. Read what he wrote in the text below.

Romans 10:1-3

1 Brethren, my heart's desire and prayer to God for Israel is, that they might be saved.
2 For I bear them record that they have a zeal of God, but not according to knowledge.
3 For they being ignorant of God's righteousness, and going about to establish their own righteousness, have not submitted themselves unto the righteousness of God.

Their problem is clearly stated in verse three. They did not know God in His righteousness, but refusing to submit to God they went on, by their own works, attempting to establish their own goodness or righteousness through obedience to the Law.

Paul's statement shows that Judaism was out of step with God and was unable to discern God at work among them. For most, zeal for God was based on a faulty premise. However God, in His faithfulness, preserved a remnant according to His purposes. Those who spiritually perceived the Truth believed; they turned to Christ and became Christians. But, unwittingly, the vast majority held fast to their unbelief. Paul describes the situation in our text.

We must remember Paul was addressing believers at Rome and all generations that follow. Notice the concern in the phrase: *For I would not, brethren, that ye should be ignorant of this mystery.* The blindness and hardened hearts of Israelwere no doubt the work of their own unbelief (2 Corinthians

4:4). But God used it as a means to support His plan for the ages.

All through the book of Acts, Luke records Paul going first to the Jewish synagogue in every city, town, and village he visited. His purpose was to persuade those who would hear him that the Messiah had arrived and His name was Jesus. He proved through the Scriptures that only Jesus could have fulfilled the details related in the prophecies.

The apostles and the followers of Jesus were driven out of Judaism. They were not allowed to be a sect or part of the religious system of the Jews like the Pharisees, Essenes, and Sadducees. Christians were considered heretics. Paul made every attempt to reach out to his Jewish brethren. Most turned a deaf ear and repeatedly sought to have him killed.

In studying the book of Acts, one discerns a distinct transition away from the unbelief of Judaism to a new entity made up of believers from Jews and Gentiles. This new sect of Judaism became known as Christ's Church. After this transition, Paul only mentions the Jews as an evangelistic priority in his letter to the Romans. He turned to the Gentiles and became their apostle.

It appears that for this season in human history, God has shifted His message of mercy and grace from the Jews to the Gentiles.

Exhortation

Israel had made a religion out of their own traditions and false concepts of God. Instead of relying on His revelation they leaned on their own traditions. It is easy for any generation of people, who have a nugget of Truth and reinterpret it, to fall into a similar trap. The process is simple; the Truth, once held in trust, is diminished to the point of being only partially true. Then, partial truth viewed as truth, is made into a golden calf and worshipped like an idol.

Be forewarned, we must worship the Source of Truth not the Truth itself. For example, Christians do not worship the Holy Bible; we worship God who reveals Himself in the Bible. We not only observe His fingerprint through the Bible, but also in our conscience and in His creation.

When the *fullness of the Gentiles* is complete, Israel will abandon her unbelief and return to Jehovah the God of her fathers. She will recognize Jesus as her Messiah and will preach Him among all nations. Meanwhile, Israel at large remains blind to the good news. The good news is that out of every generation God reserves to Himself a remnant that has not bowed the knee to Satan's lies depicted in the world system of greedy materialism and man's inhumane treatment of his fellowman.

Satan and his demons present the temptation to abandon God's Truth in many subtle ways. The enemy's ploys are too numerous to count. Couple that fact with the reality that man has a tendency to rationalize away the teaching of Scripture, and you have a ticking time bomb of potential heresy. It is not only rebellion against God, but it is also the destruction of the moral fiber of civilized society. Man is self destructing at every turn. It may well be that the previous statement is the path every spiritual error has followed.

This is my personal experience. The less time I spend with God the greater is my tendency to explain away or justify my neglect of His Word.

Therefore when I neglect prayer and meditation on the Word, I increase my likelihood for error and heretical activity.

At first, the deviation from Truth is subtle. But as the error is practiced, it becomes easier to further the deviation, until Truth is hardly discernible. Paul warns his followers not to gloat over the blindness of Israel. Why? Because while their unbelief becomes our opportunity to hear God and believe, we too can fall prey to unbelief. There can be no doubt; unbelief is the source of all spiritual blindness and hardness of heart toward God.

Questions for Discussion

1. Why did Israel reject Jesus as the Messiah?

2. What does God call those out of every generation who refuse to believe Satan's lie? Why is this significant?

3. Why does the writer say Christians do not worship the Bible?

4. When will Israel's blindness end? What will be the result of her faithfulness in the end of time?

Chapter 7

The Mystery Of
The Rapture

Chuck Missler, Bible teacher and founder of Koinonia House, said: *The doctrine of the rapture is the most preposterous teaching of the Church.* He was not being critical but simply admitting how incredulous it sounds to the unbeliever and perhaps even Christians not well taught in the Scriptures.

The word *rapture* like *trinity* is not found in our English Bible. But the concept is clearly taught by Paul as one of the secrets Jesus revealed to Him. There are at least three references that teach its reality and expected experience.

For centuries successive generations of Christians have expected its reality. However it is a controversial teaching, because some segments of Christianity do not adhere to the teaching as presented here. Just because it's controversial does not mean it's not true. Scripture is the authority for what is taught. Therefore, since Paul taught about the *catching up* or *rapture* as one of the primary mysteries, we would be grossly negligent not to write of it.

Explanation

The chronology of the record is important. Why? Because it shows unity of thought that existed between John (an original apostle) and Paul who was an apostle appointed later. What John reported Jesus said, and what Paul taught were in essence the same. Paul first wrote about the rapture (to the Church) at Thessalonica in 52 AD and later to the Corinthians in 57 AD. He addressed the issue of what would happen when Christ comes to receive his Church unto Himself.

Paul became aware of a great concern in Thessalonica. The concern regarded believers who had died in the Lord. The concern was that those asleep in Christ would not receive the same blessings as those who were alive when He came for them. There was some confusion about what Paul had taught and about what would happen when Christ comes for the Church. The issue was so important that he wrote of it in some detail to the churches in Thessalonica and Corinth.

In his epistles Paul seeks to calm their fears by reviewing with them exactly what will happen.

Please take note of this fact: Only John records a Gospel reference to the rapture event. He wrote his Gospel in 85 AD. He was the only writer that recorded Jesus' promise (John 14:1-3). The *when* of John's writing his Gospel is important! Why? Because he wrote it about twenty years after the last epistle written by Paul.

Why is the above reference to time important? Because John and other leaders would have had time to evaluate Paul's doctrine. Since Paul was the last apostle and formerly a fanatical persecutor of believers there had to be time for evaluation of his teaching. He was appointed under unusual conditions and some leaders likely had viewed him with cautious suspicion. After the Holy Spirit's confirmation John recorded the promise Jesus made about preparing a place in heaven and returning for those who believe in Him.

Those asleep in Christ would have to be resurrected. The Scriptures allude to several resurrections, and one Bible teacher counts as many as seven (the biblical number of perfection). Dr. L. S. Chafer said: *Much confusion has been introduced in prophetic interpretation by the unsupported theory that all men will be raised simultaneously.*

The theory mentioned by Dr. Chafer references the belief that there will be only one *General Resurrection* at the end of time. However, the Scriptures present us with multiple resurrections.

Christ is the first to be raised from the dead who would never die again. Therefore, the resurrections that interest us are ones that usher a person into eternity. Below is a chart of resurrections that lead to eternal life or eternal death.

BIBLICAL RESURRECTIONS CHART

ORDER	REFERENCE	CLASSIFICATION	DESTINATION
1	Matt 28:1-10; Mark 16:1-8; Luke 24:1-10; John 20:1-8	Jesus Christ	Christ is the source of eternal life.
2	Matt 27:51-53	Certain OT Saints buried around Jerusalem resurrected after Christ rose.	Eternal Life
3	1 Thess 4:13-18; 1 Cor. 15: 52-58 John14:1-3	Church	Eternal Life
4	Daniel 12:1, 2	Old Testament Saints	Eternal Life
5	Rev. 20:4	Tribulation Saints	Eternal Life
6	Presumed but no Reference	Millenial Saints	Eternal Life
7	Rev 20:11-15 Jude 15	The Wicked	Eternal Death

We can find several New Testament resurrections executed by Jesus and the apostles. However one characteristic disqualifies these from our consideration. They are disqualified because each of these persons would have had to die a second time. Our interest is in what Jesus introduced: He introduced a new order of resurrection characterized as an *Eternal Resurrection*.

Let us look closely at the details.

Exposition

The *Mystery of the Rapture* has been discussed by prophecy scholars since the early days of the Church. The central idea is conveyed in the first passage we study.

In our search for understanding, we must examine the following texts:

1 Thessalonians 4:13-18

1 Corinthians 15:51-58

John 14:1-3

We consider them in the above order because it is the order in which they were written as directed by the Holy Spirit.[51] In the first reference he answers the question: What will happen when the *Rapture* takes place?

> *1 Thessalonians 4:13-18*
> *13 But I would not have you to be ignorant, brethren, concerning them which are asleep, that ye sorrow not, even as others which have no hope.*
> *14 For if we believe that Jesus died and rose again, even so them also which sleep in Jesus will God bring with him.*
> *15 For this we say unto you by the word of the Lord, that we which are alive and remain unto*

---

[51] See the appendix regarding the chronology of the writing of New Testament documents.

the coming of the Lord shall not prevent them
which are asleep.
16 For the Lord himself shall descend from
heaven with a shout, with the voice of the
archangel, and with the trump of God: and the
dead in Christ shall rise first:
17 Then we which are alive and remain shall
be caught up together with them in the clouds,
to meet the Lord in the air: and so shall we
ever be with the Lord.
18 Wherefore comfort one another with these
words.

In verse thirteen Paul deals with the ignorance of those who do not have a clear understanding of his teaching. The question swirling in the minds of grieving believers was this: when Christ comes what will happen to those believers who have already died? His motivation for writing was to relieve their misconceptions about those who have already fallen asleep in Christ.

In verses fourteen through seventeen Paul provides a detailed description of what will happen when the Lord chooses to come. Below is a list of the progressive actions that believers may anticipate when Christ raptures the Church. All that follows are based on the Biblical reality of Christ's resurrection.

1. Christ will bring with Him the souls of all those who belong to Him (those who have died since His resurrection - vs 14).

2. Those believers alive when He comes will not have an advantage over those who sleep because the bodies of those who sleep are raised to reunite with their souls and changed into an eternal body - vs 15. (Therefore, the

living will not have an advantage over those who sleep.)

3. When Christ descends from heaven He will be announced by the voice of an archangel - vs 16a.

4. The trumpet of God will sound -vs 16b. (It does not appear that anyone will hear except those belonging to Christ.)

5. Upon the sound of the trumpet the dead in Christ will rise first - vs 16c.

6. The Scripture states that after the raising of believers who now sleep, those who remain and are alive will rise to meet the Lord in the air - vs 17a.[52]

7. All resurrected and raptured saints will begin their eternity with Christ and will never be separated from Him again - vs 17b.

Paul instructed believers to encourage one another with these triumphant Truths - vs 18. Now we glean from Paul's instruction to the church at Corinth.

> *1 Corinthians 15:51-58*
> *51 Behold, I shew you a mystery; We shall not all sleep, but we shall all be changed,*
> *52 In a moment, in the twinkling of an eye, at the last trump: for the trumpet shall sound, and the dead shall be raised incorruptible, and we shall be changed.*
> *53 For this corruptible must put on incorruption, and this mortal must put on*

---

[52] It is common knowledge among Greek language scholars that the word Rapture is from the Latin translation (rapturo) of the Greek verb rendered *caught up.*

immortality.

54 So when this corruptible shall have put on incorruption, and this mortal shall have put on immortality, then shall be brought to pass the saying that is written, Death is swallowed up in victory.

55 O death, where is thy sting? O grave, where is thy victory?

56 The sting of death is sin; and the strength of sin is the law.

In the second reference Paul answers the question: Why is a *rapture resurrection* necessary? In verse fifty-one, Paul writes about needing to be changed, this reminds us of his instruction where he said: . . . *flesh and blood cannot inherit the Kingdom of Heaven* (1 Corinthians 15:50).

The exposition begins by his announcing that whether dead or alive when Christ comes all believers will all have to be changed. In verses fifty-three and fifty-four he explains what must happen. He says the dead (whose bodies are corrupted) must now be changed so that they are incorruptible. Also those who are alive must be changed from mortal to immortality. When the above is accomplished we will be fit for heaven. He answers our question by telling us that an eternal and supernatural change must take place to make us fit for heaven. Why? Because no one can enter heaven in a physical state of flesh and blood. The change takes place in the *blink of an eye.*

Now let us focus on our next passage.

John 14:1-3

1 Let not your heart be troubled: ye believe in God, believe also in me.

2 In my Father's house are many mansions: if it were not so, I would have told you. I go to

prepare a place for you.
3 And if I go and prepare a place for you, I will come again, and receive you unto myself; that where I am, there ye may be also.

Here the apostle John encourages his readers with the words he had heard from the Master's lips. These words fell upon the disciples ears when Jesus was near the end of His earthly ministry. He was preparing them for His own death. Although His words were received when they were in a state of denial He continued His message.

What Jesus was saying disagreed with all they had been taught in the synagogue. The information they were receiving from the Lord Jesus was unbelievable. Why? Because it did not fit what they had believed their prophets had taught about Him. They had had different expectations of their Messiah. They were expecting Him to share His plans about how He would deliver Israel from foreign powers and how He would fulfill the promise that He would occupy the throne of David.

But that was not what they were hearing. Instead, He was talking about dying. Jesus was preparing them for His crucifixion. Although they were confused at that moment, the Holy Spirit would soon enable them to understand these words and much, much, more.

The passage answers the question: What is Jesus doing while we wait for Him? In these verses the Lord informs His disciples of three facts that would later be reinforced by Paul's testimony about the *mysteries* Jesus revealed to him.

There are three things Jesus told His disciples.

1. The Father has a place of dwelling (*In my Father's house are many mansions*).

2. He is preparing a place for His people (*I go to prepare a place for you*).

3. He is coming to receive them to Himself (*I will come again, and receive you unto myself; that where I am, there ye may be also*).

The above three facts relate to the rapture. Why? Because this particular set of promises was made to the apostles who became the foundations of the Church, with Christ being the cornerstone.

Exhortation

I have saved the last verses of 1 Corinthians 15 for this section on encouragement.

Please read them meditatively.

> *1 Corinthians 15:57-58*
> *57 But thanks be to God, which giveth us the victory through our Lord Jesus Christ.*
> *58 Therefore, my beloved brethren, be ye stedfast, unmoveable, always abounding in the work of the Lord, forasmuch as ye know that your labour is not in vain in the Lord.*

As we anticipate the Lord coming for us and calling us to join Him in the air, we are to be engaged in His service. Our service for Him is making disciples and teaching them to observe what Christ taught. The manner in which we are to do this is found in the verses above. Focus on the words *victory, stedfast, unmovable,* and *abounding.* These words inform us how we are to conduct ourselves as we watch for His coming.

1. **Victory**: We are victorious over the world that shows itself to us as a system of greed and hunger for power over others. We are

victorious over the flesh with its many illegitimate desires. Also, we are victorious over the *devil,* who Christ defeated for us on the cross. Therefore we must give our service to Him in a triumphant manner with humility that avoids arrogance.

2. **Steadfast:** We are to be steadfast without being obstinate. Steadfastness is sticking to the task without being deterred by obstacles or distractions. We are to keep at the task depending on His enabling strength.

3. **Unmovable**: We will, by God's grace, stay on our course. We will not be persuaded by the philosophies of men. Human philosophies tend to weaken the resolve of those seeking to remain faithful to Christ.

4. **Bounding**: We are bounding in our spirit with the certainty of His Truth driving us to faithfulness. As a dog gleefully and dutifully bounds to retrieve a stick thrown by his master, so we with a bountiful and worshipful spirit, commit ourselves to the Lord's service.

With these four exhortations in place, every succeeding generation of believers will work and watch until Jesus comes.

Questions for Discussion

1. Define the term *rapture* and *caught up* as recorded in 1 Thessalonians 4:17.

2. How many possible resurrections are there that have eternal consequences?

3. What are the four things Paul exhorts Christians to do while waiting for Christ to come?

4. Do you believe in the rapture of the Church? If so why and if not why?

Chapter 8

The Mystery
Of Iniquity

The mystery of iniquity doth already work.

2 Thessalonians 2:7

Man has experienced the presence of evil ever since the failure of Adam in Eden's garden. Everyone knows evil's reality. From the very moment we become aware of life, we are aware of evil as an influence. It permeates man and his social environment.[53]

---

[53] We resist the temptation to get involved in a philosophical discussion about the origin of evil and whether or not God sanctioned it.

However that does not mean man is inherently devoid of value. God created man in His image.[54] But in his present state, man is separated from God with no hope of self-recovery. Adam's refusal to obey God in the garden resulted in all mankind being cursed with Adam's nature. Man inherited his desire to sin from Adam. The desire is called the *sin nature*. Therefore, we do not sin to become sinners, we sin because we are sinners.

God in His mercy has provided a second Adam who is His Son. He will give a new birth, a new family and a new spiritual identity to anyone who believes in His Son.

Explanation

Evil forces have been at work in every generation seeking to thwart the work of God. Through the centuries, the purposes of God have had major successes. For example I would cite two periods, the first from the resurrection of Christ until about 300 AD, and from the reformation until World War I. However, as we move into the early years of the twenty-first century, science has replaced God as man's authority. Crime is increasing as our society loses its respect for law. There is evidence of encroaching chaos in almost every arena of society.

The study of the *Mystery of Iniquity* is against a backdrop of increasing lawlessness and open rebellion against biblical morality. Satan and his demonic hordes have worked tirelessly in every

---

[54] For a fuller discussion see *Our Unseen Enemy* or *What Jesus Taught* by William L. Owens.

generation since being exiled from heaven (Revelation 12:4).[55]

Before the world was created God found iniquity in Lucifer's heart. It was Satan's intention to conduct a supernatural coup; he determined to usurp God's authority (Ezekiel 28:17). God had entrusted him with guardianship of His throne. It is referred to as the Mountain of God in Ezekiel 28:16. Somehow Lucifer deceived himself into thinking his intelligence and supernatural powers were such that he could overthrow God, and rob Him of His glory. His arrogance and pride are seen in the multiple use of his declarations regarding what he planned to do. Read the account in Isaiah 14.

> *Isaiah 14:12-14*
> *12 How art thou fallen from heaven, O Lucifer, son of the morning! How art thou cut down to the ground, which didst weaken the nations!*
> *13 For thou hast said in thine heart, I will ascend into heaven, I will exalt my throne above the stars of God:*
> *I will sit also upon the mount of the congregation, in the sides of the north:*
> *14 I will ascend above the heights of the clouds; I will be like the most High.*

Notice in Isaiah's record the personal pronoun *I*. These pronouns declare the five things Lucifer plans to accomplish.

1. I will ascend into heaven.

2. I will exalt my throne above the stars of God.

---

[55] It is not clear if the Revelation verse takes place in the great tribulation or is a vision of what had already happened before time began. We know Lucifer's exile was partial because Job records him reporting to the Lord asking for permission for what he does (Job 1:6-12; 2:1-8).

3. I will sit also upon the mount of the congregation, in the sides of the north.

4. I will ascend above the heights of the clouds.

5. I will be like the most High.

One does not need an imagination to see that Lucifer's goal has been to take control of God's kingdom. However, God saw the iniquity in Lucifer's heart and cast him down to the earth along with the rebellious angels that followed Lucifer. While Lucifer has been judged, he has not thus far experienced the full fury of his sentence. His sentence will be solemnly executed at the final judgment when he and his angels will be cast into the Lake of Fire for an eternity of torment (Revelation 20:10).

Christ had ascended into heaven leaving us with the command to make disciples. But there was the awaited promise that He would come again. The disciples had heard that there were those claiming Christ's coming to be at hand. Paul takes up his pen to correct this false teaching. He knew the lie was one of Satan's ploys.

Exposition

Until God brings history to a close, Satan is allowed to exercise his iniquities and wicked strategies attempting to disrupt God's plan for restoring His glory.

Well, we ask, what does this have to do with the mystery of iniquity? To answer that question we will do well to examine our text.

2 Thessalonians 2:1-12

1 Now we beseech you, brethren, by the coming of our Lord Jesus Christ, and by our gathering together unto him,

2 That ye be not soon shaken in mind, or be troubled, neither by spirit, nor by word, nor by letter as from us, as that the day of Christ is at hand.

3 Let no man deceive you by any means: for that day shall not come, except there come a falling away first, and that man of sin be revealed, the son of perdition;

4 Who opposeth and exalteth himself above all that is called God, or that is worshipped; so that he as God sitteth in the temple of God, shewing himself that he is God.

5 Remember ye not, that, when I was yet with you, I told you these things?

6 And now ye know what withholdeth that he might be revealed in his time.

7 For the mystery of iniquity doth already work: only he who now letteth will let, until he be taken out of the way.

8 And then shall that qWicked be revealed, whom the Lord shall consume with the spirit of his mouth, and shall destroy with the brightness of his coming:

9 Even him, whose coming is after the working of Satan with all power and signs and lying wonders,

10 And with all deceivableness of unrighteousness in them that perish; because they received not the love of the truth, that they might be saved.

11 And for this cause God shall send them strong delusion, that they should believe a lie:

12 That they all might be damned who

believed not the truth, but had pleasure in unrighteousness.

It is not certain what happened to cause confusion regarding a false prophecy about the *Day of the Christ.*

Paul had carefully taught them about the coming of Christ for His people. He taught them that before God's wrath is poured out on earth, Christ would come for those trusting in His Word. Some misinformation about Paul's teaching had caused confusion. There was either some teacher, some word of gossip, or maybe some circulating letter that was supposedly from Paul, informing them that the day of the Lord had begun. Paul corrects the error and provides specific instruction about what to expect.

Paul begins by expressing concern that someone had confused them about when Christ would return to judge the world. He seeks to allay their troubled hearts by letting them know that there are certain things that must take place before Christ comes to judge.

First, we will observe the *mystery of iniquity* continually at work with an ebb and flow over time (vs. 7a). One translation of the word *iniquity* is *lawlessness.* Satan's strategy is to spread sedition and rebellion. He is the author of anarchy.

Paul observed the devil at work on his missionary journeys. He taught disciples to expect to be persecuted by people who were being energized by demonic forces. Through the centuries we have continued to observe the persecution of Christians. In some countries the persecution is physical while in others it is spiritual and emotional. True followers of Christ are struggling to resist the waves of evil expressed in every imaginable way. Be thankful to God for His grace and that it is sufficient for every trial.

Second, the One who currently restrains wickedness must be removed before He will come to judge (vs. 7b). In this verse the apostle informs us about *the restrainer of sin.* Paul said the *day of the Lord* will not come until the restrainer is *taken out of the way.* Over the centuries, commentators have deliberated about the identification of the restrainer. The only explanation that satisfies most believers is that He is the Holy Spirit. Some object saying it cannot be the Holy Spirit, because He is God and He is in the world and is present everywhere. Therefore He cannot be removed. While that is true, He can remove Himself. How? By removing His Church through which He is presently restraining evil.

He is currently indwelling His people the Church. As salt retards corruption, the church retards evil by her presence in the world. When Christ raptures the Church, the Holy Spirit will in effect be taken out of the way, but He will still be present.

Thirdly, the man of sin is revealed (vs. 8). Paul reminds the Church that a spiritual leader will emerge out of the masses. He will be Satan's man. The devil will stand behind him energizing his every action. The masses will be deceived by his miracle working power. People will turn to him as if he were God. The Truth of God will be mocked and they will not hear the Truth that they may be saved (vs. 8-10). This man must be revealed before the Lord will come the second time in judgment.

It only then that the Lord Jesus will come in glory to judge the nations and set up His millennial kingdom (2 Thessalonians 1:7, 8). He will come as King and Judge at the end of a seven year period known as the *great tribulation*. Paul warned the Church at Thessalonica not to listen to false reports. Why? Because no man or angel knows when Jesus is coming.

Exhortation

Iniquity abounds and will continue until it is curbed and finally stopped by the triumphant return of the Savior. The devil does not know when Christ will return. No one in heaven or earth knows except the Father. However, we intuitively know it will be soon. I suppose all successive generations of believers have expected His coming in their lifetime.

Satan also senses his time is short and he will not quit. For whatever reason, Satan still believes he can win. The devil and his angels are delusional, like many in our world today. Sadly they are carrying vast numbers of deceived souls with them into the eternal fires of torment.

How then shall we live in expectation of the restrainer being taken out of the way? We must in due diligence remain resolute in our commitment to do His will, determined in our dependence on the Holy Spirit's enabling power, and draw our strength from prayerful meditation on Scripture. In a practical manner we must love the Lord our God with all our body, soul, and spirit and love others as we love ourselves.

Remember, Jesus is coming and He is victorious. At the end of His millennial reign (from the throne of David) He will bring all time to a close.

The Scriptures predict the restoration of all His creation to its former glory. God will destroy sin and all judgments will be completed at the Great White Throne (Revelation 21:1-22:21).

The earth will be filled with the joy of the Lord. All creatures great and small will glorify the presence of the Lord. The New Jerusalem is prepared for those who love Him. We will live forever, doing what will never be a burden to us and where no need will ever go unmet. We will spend eternity with our Savior whom we will never grow weary of adoring. We will eternally learn, growing in both knowledge and wisdom. Heaven will be where boredom is not known.

To God be the Glory! Amen!

Questions for Discussion

1.   What is the *mystery of iniquity?*

2.   Why were the believers in Thessalonica confused about the *day of the Lord*?

3.   What are the things Paul said had to happen before the second coming of Christ?

4.   How should we live as we await Christ's coming?

Chronology Chart of New Testament Books

(Dates are Approximate)

BOOK	YEAR WRITTEN	BOOK	YEAR WRITTEN
James	50 AD	Ephesians	62 AD
Mark	50 AD	I Peter	62 AD
I Thessalonians	52 AD	II Peter	65 AD
II Thessalonians	52 AD	Jude	67 AD
I Corinthians	57 AD	Titus	67 AD
II Corinthians	57 AD	I Timothy	67 AD
Galatians	58 AD	II Timothy	68 AD
Romans	58 AD	Hebrews	69 AD
Matthew	58 AD	John's Gospel	85 AD
Luke	58 AD	I John	85 AD
Acts	62 AD	II John	85 AD
Philippians	62 AD	III John	85 AD
Philemon	62 AD	Revelation	95 AD
Colossians	62 AD		

New Testament Canon

In the chart below we see the final order of the Books of the NT along with their authors and the general subject of content.

After Acts, we have the instructional epistles. The first thirteen come from the pen of Paul (Romans thru Philemon), then we have Hebrews, James, I & II Peter, I-II-III John, and Jude. These twenty-one epistles form the heart of Christian instruction and have become the handbook for Christian life and work.

In the chart below we observe each book's order and date of writing. The order of writing is important to determine the nature of the message being taught by Jesus, along with the first apostles and then Paul (the last apostle).

BOOK	HUMAN AUTHOR	SUBJECT
Matthew	Matthew	Christ is presented to the Jews as their King
Mark	John Mark	Christ is presented as the servant of man.
Luke	Luke	Christ is presented as truly man.
John	John	Christ is presented as truly God.

BOOK	HUMAN AUTHOR	SUBJECT
Acts	Luke	The Holy Spirit has Luke record the history of how Christianity transitioned from Judaism.
Romans	Paul	The book is a doctrinal treatise on Christ, faith, sin and grace.
I Corinthians	Paul	Paul instructs the believers about how to function as a church and how to resolve sin issues among members.
II Corinthians	Paul	Paul continues to deal with unresolved issues and offers instruction on giving.
Galatians	Paul	Paul defends the doctrine of justification by faith and warns of Judaizers.
Ephesians	Paul	Paul teaches about the Christian's heavenly position as a member of His body.
Philippians	Paul	Paul teaches about the spiritual character of Christians who walk in the Spirit.
Colossians	Paul	Paul addresses the Christians union with Christ and warns about false religious practices.
I Thessalonians	Paul:	The Holy Spirit has Paul clarify some issues about the end-time and the coming again of Christ.

BOOK	HUMAN AUTHOR	SUBJECT
II Thessalonians	Paul:	Paul revisits the end-times issue and also writes about *the man of sin.* He adds instruction about Christian behavior.
I Timothy	Paul	Timothy receives instruction about how to qualify church leaders and how the church should function.
II Timothy	Paul:	Paul instructs the believers about how to be good soldiers and how to reproduce disciples through mentoring.
Titus	Paul	Paul offers more pastoral training about dealing with age groups and other essential topics.
Philemon	Paul	Onesimus, Philemon's slave, escaped and became Paul's helper. Paul introduced him to Christ and writes a letter to Philemon appealing to him to receive Onesimus as a Christian brother.
Hebrews	Unknown (Tradition has Paul as author.)	The book is filled with contrasting arguments. Jewish believers are urged to remain faithful to Christ who has revealed Himself as God's Son.

BOOK	HUMAN AUTHOR	SUBJECT
James	James	James challenges believers to be faithful to the teachings of his half-brother Jesus. He argues faith is revealed by one's behavior.
I Peter	Peter	Peter writes chiefly about the grace of God working in the believer's life.
II Peter	Peter	Peter writes about how to live in the last days as we wait for the advent of the Lord.
I John	John	John tells his disciples about God's remedy for dealing with known sin.
II John	John	John focuses on two issues: love for one another and anti-Christian teachers.
III John	John	John charges his disciples to walk in Truth.
Jude	Jude	Jude challenges believers to defend the faith in the face of apostasy.
Revelation	John	John writes his revelation from Christ about how God will bring about His ultimate will in restoring His glory and destroying all evil.

The chart above reflects the final order of NT books as decided by the church councils in the first four centuries. My view of Scripture causes me to believe that the Holy Spirit not only wrote the original text by moving upon holy men by using their own personalities. I also believe He superintended the arrangement of their final order by superintending the various church councils.

To understand the Bible one would do well to recognize the classification and purpose of each book. For example the synoptic Gospels are Matthew, Mark, and Luke. Their purpose is primarily historical. They tell the story of Jesus' life, death, and resurrection. [56]

John's Gospel is uniquely different. It was the last Gospel written and its purpose was to present Jesus as deity. It clearly declares Jesus to be the Son of God. Matthew wrote to show Jesus was the King of the Jews. Mark purposed in his Gospel to present Jesus as man's servant. Luke wrote to prove that Jesus was indeed a man. The claims of Matthew, Mark, and Luke were somewhat acceptable to the Jewish establishment, as long as you recognized Jesus as a teacher and not the Messiah. However, John's claim Jesus is divine was an affront to the Jewish mind. Why? Because they clearly understood from their culture, that to claim to be the Son of God was actually a claim to be equal with God. They rejected the doctrine of the

---

[56] When interpreting the Scriptures, you will do well to understand them literally or plainly. Avoid using types and metaphors unless the Scriptures themselves do so. Keep these three entities separate: Israel, the Gentiles, and the Church. There is no evidence Jesus' first disciples ever intended to separate themselves from their Jewish roots or the teachings of Moses. They were driven out of Judaism because of their insistence that Jesus is the Messiah.

incarnation. They did not believe God could humiliate Himself to become a man. But that is exactly what He did!

Following the Gospels, *Acts of the Apostles* records what the apostles accomplished through the Holy Spirit after Jesus' resurrection. Beginning with Christ's ascension into heaven, Acts contains the story of how Christianity transitioned from a Jewish sect into a separate entity called *the Church*.

In The New Testament library, there are some sections of prophecy, but the book of Revelation is the only one designated a prophetic book. It tells us about the future destruction and restoration of the heavens and the earth. It is the record of God's final victory over evil and His judgment on Satan, his demons (fallen angels) and unrepentant sinners.[57] He also records the restoration of all His creation to its former glory.

---

[57] The writer believes *demons* and *fallen angels* are different terms for the same entity. But some believe them to be two separate beings that have followed Satan in his rebellion against God (Isaiah 14; Ezekiel 28; Revelation 12).

TIMELINE FOR THE APOSTLE PAUL

(A Timeline of Approximate Dates)

AD 2-5   Saul is born in Tarsus.

AD 5-22   Saul was reared in Tarsus of Cilicia.

AD 22-32   Saul was educated in Jerusalem under Gamaliel.

AD 32   Saul encouraged the stoning of Stephen.

AD 33/34   Saul is converted on the road to Damascus (Acts 9:1-9).

AD 33/34   The Holy Spirit heals Saul through Ananias (Acts 9:10-19).

AD 33-35   Saul becomes Paul and retreats into Arabia (Gal. 1:17).

AD 35   Paul makes his 1st post conversion visit to Jerusalem (Acts 9:26-29).

AD 35/36   Paul leaves Jerusalem and goes back to Tarsus (Acts 9:29-30).

AD 35/36   Paul visits Syria and Cilicia (Gal. 1:21-24).

AD 40   Paul accompanies Barnabas to Antioch (Acts 11:25-26)

AD 42   Agabus predicts famine for Jerusalem (Acts 11:27-29)

AD 42, 43 Paul and Barnabas carry famine relief to Judea (Acts 11:30; 12:25).

AD 46-48 **PAUL'S FIRST MISSION JOURNEY**

Cyprus

Paul and Barnabas preach at Salamis (Acts 13:4-5).

Paul blinds Elymas the Magician for his disrespect for holy things (Acts 13: 6-12).

Perga:

John Mark leaves the mission (Acts 12:13; 15:38).

Antioch of Pisidia

Paul preaches in the Synagogue (Acts:13: 14-43). The Jews are threatened by Paul's preaching (Acts 13:44-49).

Paul and Barnabas are driven out (Acts 13:50-51).

Iconium:

Paul and Barnabas visit Iconium (Acts 14:1-6; 2 Timothy 3:11).

Lystra

Paul heals a man at Lystra (Acts 14:8-18).

Paul is stoned at Lystra (Acts 14:19-20).

Derbe

Paul and Barnabas preached at Derbe (Acts 14:20-21).

Antioch of Pisidia

Paul and Barnabas return to Antioch and report to the church all they had experienced on their journey (Acts 14:26-28).

AD 48 THE JERUSALEM COUNCIL
(Acts 15:1-21)

Paul and Barnabas go to Jerusalem to settle the argument with Judaizers who demanded that Gentile converts be circumcised and obey the laws of Moses (Acts 15:1-5).

Peter states his case against Judaizers (Acts 15:6-11).

Paul and Barnabas offer closing testimony of what God had done for the Gentiles. (Acts 15:12).

Pastor James announces the decision of the council (Acts 15:13-22).

The council sends letters by Judas and Silas to the Gentile believers at Antioch announcing those receiving Christ are not under the Law (Acts 15:19-34).

Paul and Barnabas return to Antioch to teach (Acts15:35).

Paul writes 1 Thessalonians AD 40-50

AD 49/51 PAUL'S SECOND MISSION JOURNEY

Paul and Barnabas separate over John Mark (Acts 15:36-18:22).

Paul and Silas go through Syria and Cilicia strengthening the churches (Acts 15:40-41).

Paul and Silas go to Derbe and Lystra where they find a faithful disciple named Timothy (Acts 16:1-5).

Paul and Silas go to Troas — Paul has a vision of a Macedonian asking for help (Acts 16:6-10).

Paul and Silas sail to Neapolis and go to Philippi where they meet Lydia; she and her household are saved (Acts 16:11-15).

Paul and Silas are thrown into jail (Acts16:16-25).

An earthquake frees them. Paul and Silas witness to the jailer; he and his household are saved. (Acts 16:25-34)

Paul and Silas preach in the synagogue at Thessalonica and many are saved (Acts 17:1-10).

They flee to Berea and continue to preach.

Paul goes to Athens while Timothy and Silas remain in Berea.

Paul sends word for them to join him.

Paul preaches at Athens — many men and women come to Christ (Acts 17:16-34).

Paul goes to Corinth where Timothy and Silas join him, and they teach the Word for 18 months Acts 18:1-17).

Paul writes 2 Thessalonians

Paul returns to Antioch of Syria with stops at Ephesus, Caesarea, and Jerusalem (Acts 18:18-22).

AD 53-55

Paul writes Galatians, 1 Corinthians, Philemon, and Philippians.

AD 54-58   PAUL'S THIRD MISSION JOURNEY

Paul travels through Galatia and Phrygia (Acts 18:23). At Ephesus, Paul encounters some disciples who have not received the Holy Spirit but have only received John's baptism (Acts 19:1-7).

(Timothy is sent to Corinth (1 Corinthians 4:17). He returns to Ephesus later (1 Corinthians 16:10-11).

Paul preaches in the synagogue for 3 months and then at the school of Tyrannus for 2 years (Acts 9:8-10).

He sends Timothy and Erastus into Macedonia Acts 19:21).

On his way to Macedonia Paul stops at Troas hoping to meet with Titus (Acts 20:1, 2 Corinthians 2:13).

Philippi is probably the place where he finally meets with Titus and from here he writes 2 Corinthians.

He sends Titus to Corinth with his second letter (2 Corinthians 7:6, 8:6, Acts 20:2).

Paul goes to Greece for 3 months and writes the book of Romans (Acts 20:2-3).

From Greece, Timothy and other brethren go ahead of Paul planning to meet at Troas (Acts 20:4-6).

Paul goes to Troas and stays 7 days where he partakes in the Lord's Supper (Acts 20:7-12).

Paul travels to Assos by foot and sails to Mitylene, Chios, Samos, Trogyllium, and stops at Miletus (Acts 20:13-16).

Paul sends for the Ephesian leaders, and he exhorts them to be faithful to serve God's flock (Acts 20:17-38).

Paul sails to Cos, Rhodes, Patara, and the party stops at Tyre for 7 days (Acts 21:3-6).

He stays at Ptolemais for one day (Acts 21:7).

Paul travels to Caesarea—he stays with Philip the evangelist (Acts 21:8-14).

AD 58–68 PAUL'S FINAL JOURNEY

Paul goes to Jerusalem and is arrested in the temple because his preaching causes a riot (Acts 21: 15-36).

He is allowed to address the mob (Acts 21:37 – 22:21).

He speaks to the Sanhedrin Council (Acts 22:30–23:10).

Certain zealous Jews plot to kill Paul; they take an oath not to eat or drink until they kill him(Acts 23:12-23).

Paul is sent to Caesarea to appear before governor Felix (Acts 23: 23-25).

Paul gives his defense before Felix (Acts 24:10-27).

Paul Speaks before Festus and appeals to Caesar (Acts 25:1-12).

He gives his testimony before King Agrippa
(Acts 25:13–26:32).

Paul, as a prisoner, is sent to Rome that he
may plead his case before Caesar (Acts 27:1-2).

At Sidon, Paul gets to visit with his friends
and then continues to Myra (Acts 27:3-5).

They change boats and sail to Fair Havens (Acts
27:6-8).

Against Paul's warnings, they set sail for
Phoenix. A strong wind comes through and
forces them by Clauda and then out to sea
until they are shipwrecked at Malta
(Acts 27:9–28:1).

At Malta Paul survives a viper bite and heals
many of the natives over the next 3 months
(Acts 28:2-10).

From there, they sail to Syracuse and stay for
3 days (Acts 28:11-12).

They sail to Rhegium and then to Pateoli
where he was allowed to stay 7 days with his
brethren (Acts 28:13).

At Rome, Paul stayed for 2 years under house
arrest in his own rented house where he
could receive visitors and preach the word
(Acts 28: 17-31).

Paul writes Philemon, Colossians, Ephesians,
and Philippians.

Timothy is at Rome with Paul part of the time
(Philippians 1:1, Colossians 1:1).

Timothy was in prison at some point during
this time (Hebrews 13:23).

Paul, as anticipated, is released from his first Roman imprisonment (Philippians 1:22; 2:19-24).

He possibly goes to Spain (Romans 15:28).

Paul goes to Crete where he leaves Titus to work with the church (Titus 1:5).

He travels to Miletus and possibly goes to Colossae (2 Timothy 4:20; Philemon 1:22).

Paul meets with Timothy in Ephesus and leaves him there to work with the church as he travels to Macedonia (1Timothy 1:3).

He travels to Troas where he leaves his books and cloak (2 Timothy 4:13).

Paul goes to Philippi and possible writes 1 Timothy (Philippians 2:19-24).

He possibly writes Titus on his way to Nicopolis where he planned to spend the winter. (Titus 3:12)

After 2 years or more being free, Paul is arrested a final time. Paul writes 2 Timothy which is his final letter. In it, he sends for Timothy. (2 Timothy 4:9-12)

AD 68   PAUL IS BEHEADED BY NERO

Charting The Process of Salvation and Spiritual Growth

William L. Owens

In eternity past, the self-existing God who reveals Himself as Father, Son and Spirit, created all spirit creatures such as angels who attended His pleasure. Angels were assigned their appropriate duties. One angel, whose name was Lucifer, seems to have been the guardian of God's throne (Ezekiel 28:14).

Lucifer rebelled and attempted to usurp the authority of God (Isaiah 14:12-14).

Iniquity was discovered in his heart. God judged him and cast him down to earth, and he became the *god of this world* (2 Corinthians 4:4), but his ultimate judgment is eternal damnation (Matthew 25:41; Revelation 12:7-12).

We are not given the details of creation other than earth. (It is possible that God created other planets, galaxies, and universes before or at the time He created earth - Genesis 1:1).

God created Earth, all living creatures, and a man named Adam (Genesis 1:2-2:20).

God created a woman out of Adam and she was named Eve (Genesis 3:20).

God created a perfect garden in Eden and instructed Adam and Eve to tend it and to eat of the trees in the garden for their nourishment (Genesis 2:8-16).

However, there was one exception; they could not eat of the tree of knowledge of good and evil or they would die (Genesis 2:17).

The serpent came into the garden and tempted Eve to eat of the forbidden tree. He suggested she would not die, but would be like God, knowing good and evil (Genesis 3:1-5).

Seeing the fruit was good to eat and desirous, she ate and invited Adam to eat and he ate. Eve was deceived but Adam was not (Genesis 3:6).

When Adam and Eve ate of the tree they knew immediately they were naked and became fearful of God. Their awareness alerts us to how quickly sin affects one's life. They also died spiritually being separated from God's fellowship (Genesis 3:7-19).

God's judgment on sin quickly followed; He judged the serpent (Satan) for tempting Eve; He judged Eve for not believing God's instructions; He judged Adam for disobedience (Genesis 3:14-19).

The rebellion did not take God by surprise. God the Son had agreed in eternity past to pay for the sins of the world by dying as a sacrificial Lamb for sin (Revelation 13:8).

Adam and Eve tried to cover their nakedness with fig leaves and hid from God among the trees (Genesis 3:7). (Their action was apparently unacceptable to God.)

God restored fellowship with Adam and Eve by providing them animal skins to cover their nakedness (Genesis 3:21; Hebrews 9:22). (The skins represented the shedding of blood for their sins.)

Because of the testimony of Jesus, we now know the skins were a foreshadow of His death as a sacrificial Lamb in human history for the sins of the world (John 3:16).

The disobedience of the first human parents removed innocence from the human spirit so that all descendants of Adam and Eve are born with a nature that has a natural tendency to sin (Romans 6:23).

Salvation is revealed to be a three step process. (God has chosen to save all who believe His witness by justifying, sanctifying and glorifying them.)

Step 1: Justification

Justification takes place when one believes in Christ as personal Savior. Because Christ died for the sins of the world, the Father pronounces believers justified and saved from His wrath on sin.

Failure of the First Adam Dooms All

Adam, the 1st man was a created being (Genesis 2:7).

He was tempted by Satan to believe God's forbidding them to eat the fruit from the tree of knowledge was not for their benefit (Genesis 3:5).

Adam sinned by not obeying God; Eve sinned because her flesh desired the fruit and because she believed Satan's lie. She yielded to her desire and partook of what God had forbidden (Genesis 3:6).

All mankind, as the offspring of Adam and Eve, are lost without innocence, and are rebellious toward the will of God (Romans 5:8).

In the state of our natural birth, we are in bondage to sin (Romans 8:21).

In bondage, man finds himself the servant or slave of sin (Galatians 5:1; Hebrews 2:15).

As a sinner, man is ruled by his fleshly desires.

The Law of God is a curse to him. Why? Because it condemns his behavior driven by his flesh (James 1:14, 15).

Therefore, man is lost because he is separated from God and under God's curse of both physical and spiritual death (Romans 3:23). (There is no evidence that death existed before Adam sinned.)

Success of the Second Adam Saves All Believers

The 2nd Adam (Jesus) was the only begotten Son of God (John 3:16). He has always existed; He was not created; He was incarnated in human flesh (John 1:14). Jesus is the only Son (born of His seed) God has ever had.

He was tempted in His humanity to sin against the Father, but He refused to do so (Luke 4:1-13). In all His earthly life He never disobeyed; He never sinned (Hebrews 4:15).

The 2nd Adam (Jesus) was the Lamb of God who takes away the sin of the world (John 1:29).

The 2nd Adam, innocent of sin, died for all sins ever committed in the world and took upon Himself the wrath of God that we sinners deserve (1 John

2:2). (Jesus' substitutionary death for the sins of the world, satisfied God's holiness and enabled Him to grant forgiveness and mercy to those in bondage to sin.)

Christ was crucified to pay the penalty for sin; He was buried to submit to God's curse of death on those who sin; He rose showing Himself to be the source of life and victorious over sin and death (1 Corinthians 15:3-8).

God declared He would forgive all who repent and believe His good-news regarding Christ dying for the sins of the world (John 3:14-16; Romans 5:8). God restorcs the believer to a spiritual state through the *new birth* (John 3:5).

Because Christ committed Himself to the cross before the world began (Revelations 13:8), God made it possible to save believers from every generation who placed their faith in His witness (Romans 4:3; Galatians 3:6; James 2:23). (It was on this basis, that God forgave Adam and Eve, Abraham, Moses, David, etc. He forgave them on the expectation of Christ's crucifixion in earthly history.)

Step 2: Sanctification

Sanctification is an act of being set aside for God's exclusive use. There are two aspects of sanctification.

The first is known as *positional sanctification* and it takes place immediately upon trusting Christ. When one believes on Christ, the Father spiritually positions the believer alongside Christ in heaven.

The other aspect is *experiential sanctification* and is progressive in nature. It takes place over time and is completed when the Lord terminates the believers time on earth and brings him home. He will use either physical death or the rapture to bring us into His eternal presence (John 14:1-3; I Thessalonians 4:13-18).

Sanctification has only one goal: the glory of the Father through the sanctifying power of the Word (John 17:1, 17).

The Father is glorified when His children take on the spiritual likeness of His Son (2 Peter 3:18; Romans 8:28,29).

The Christian life is a series of experiences directed by God to assure the believer arrives at the desired destination of completeness in Christ (Romans 8:28, 29; Hebrews 13:20, 21).

God provides the Christian with the Holy Spirit who guides, instructs, comforts, and convicts.

The believer responds to the Holy Spirit's leadership:

1. He counts himself in the heavens with Christ (Ephesians 1:20);

2. He counts himself free from the judgment of the Law (Romans 8:1);

3. He counts himself dead to the condemning power of sin (Romans 6:6; 11);

4. He counts himself holy or perfect in Christ (James 1:4);

5. He counts himself resting in Christ (the vine) to provide him with the spiritual energy (life) to live abundantly to God's glory (John 15:5);

6. He counts himself as having God's presence when facing the trials and temptations of life (Hebrews 13:5; 1 Corinthians 10:13).

Step 3: Glorification

The Christian is glorified when he receives his spiritual body in Heaven. It is unclear as to what believers will have in the way of a body before the resurrection. Some have suggested that God will provide us with a temporary body until our resurrection.

A Chronology of
the Mystery Passages

(Using the King James Version)

William L. Owens

In the chart below you may observe the mystery or mysteries and their explanation the Holy Spirit references in the text.

Passage	King James Text	Identify the Mystery
Matt 13:11	He answered and said unto them, Because it is given unto you to know the <u>mysteries</u> of the kingdom of heaven, but to them it is not given.	The teachings of Christ are referred to as the mysteries of the Kingdom of Heaven. (See Chapter 2 of Part II.)
Mark 4:11	And he said unto them, Unto you it is given to know the <u>mystery</u> of the kingdom of God: but unto them that are without, all *these* things are done in parables:	The teachings of Christ are referred to as the mysteries of the Kingdom of Heaven. (See Chapter 2 of Part II.)

Luke 8:10	And he said, Unto you it is given to know the <u>mysteries</u> of the kingdom of God: but to others in parables; that seeing they might not see, and hearing they might not understand.	The teachings of Christ are referred to as the mysteries of the Kingdom of Heaven. (See Chapter 2 of Part II.)
Rom 11:25	For I would not, brethren, that ye should be ignorant of this <u>mystery</u>, lest ye should be wise in your own conceits; that blindness in part is happened to Israel, until the fullness of the Gentiles be come in.	The Mystery of Israel's Blindness (See Chapter 6 of Part II.)
Rom 16:25	Now to him that is of power to stablish you according to my gospel, and the preaching of Jesus Christ, according to the revelation of the <u>mystery</u>, which was kept secret since the world began,	The revelation of Jesus Christ and His Gospel is here referred to as the mystery. (See Chapter 3 of Part II.)

1 Cor 2:7	But we speak the wisdom of God in a mystery, *even* the hidden *wisdom,* which God ordained before the world unto our glory:	The teaching Paul received from Jesus is spoken of as God's wisdom. (See Chapter 2 of Part II.)
1 Cor 4:1	Let a man so account of us, as of the ministers of Christ, and stewards of the mysteries of God.	Here the word describes the responsibility of apostles, and all ministers, for they are Stewards of the Mysteries. (See Chapter 3 of Part II.)
1 Cor 13:2	And though I have *the gift of* prophecy, and understand all mysteries, and all knowledge; and though I have all faith, so that I could remove mountains, and have not charity, I am nothing.	Understanding mysteries is listed with other spiritual gifts. However, having gifts and understanding the secrets of God are nothing, if you do not exercise love. (See Chapter 3 of Part II.)
1 Cor 14:2	For he that speaketh in an *unknown* tongue speaketh not unto men, but unto God: for no man understandeth *him;* howbeit in the spirit he speaketh mysteries.	Those who speak a language unknown to his hearers sounds like he is speaking mysteries, because the hearer does not understand.

1 Cor 15:51	Behold, I shew you a <u>mystery</u>; We shall not all sleep, but we shall all be changed,	The Mystery of the Translation of the Church (See Chapter 6 of Part II.)
Eph 1:9	Having made known unto us the <u>mystery</u> of his will, according to his good pleasure which he hath purposed in himself:	What Jesus taught Paul is referred to as the Mystery of God's will as revealed by Jesus. (See Chapter 3 of Part II.)
Eph 3:3	How that by revelation he made known unto me the <u>mystery</u>; (as I wrote afore in few words,	Paul speaks of the mysteries being revealed to him by Jesus.
Eph 3:4	Whereby, when ye read, ye may understand my knowledge in the <u>mystery</u> of Christ)	Again, Paul speaks of the mysteries being revealed to him by Jesus.
Eph 3:9	And to make all *men* see what *is* the fellowship of the <u>mystery</u>, which from the beginning of the world hath been hid in God, who created all things by Jesus Christ:	Those who believe the mysteries of God form a special fellowship. It is called the Church.

Eph 5:32	This is a great mystery: but I speak concerning Christ and the church.	The Mystery of the Church (See Chapter 4 of Part II.)
Eph 6:19	And for me, that utterance may be given unto me, that I may open my mouth boldly, to make known the mystery of the gospel,	The Mystery of the Gospel (See Chapter 3 of Part II.)
Col 1:26	*Even* the mystery which hath been hid from ages and from generations, but now is made manifest to his saints:	The mystery of God is now revealed through Christ unto Paul.
Col 1:27	To whom God would make known what *is* the riches of the glory of this mystery among the Gentiles; which is Christ in you, the hope of glory:	The Mystery of the Indwelling Christ

Col 2:2	That their hearts might be comforted, being knit together in love, and unto all riches of the full assurance of understanding, to the acknowledgement of the mystery of God, and of the Father, and of Christ;	Understanding the Mysteries brings comfort, assurance and a special bond through faith in God through Christ.
Col 4:3	Withal praying also for us, that God would open unto us a door of utterance, to speak the mystery of Christ, for which I am also in bonds:	The mystery of God is now revealed through Christ unto Paul.
2 Thess 2:7	For the mystery of iniquity doth already work: only he who now letteth *will let*, until he be taken out of the way.	The Mystery of Iniquity
1 Tim 3:9	Holding the mystery of the faith in a pure conscience.	The Mystery of the Faith

1 Tim 3:16	And without controversy great is the <u>mystery</u> of godliness: God was manifest in the flesh, justified in the Spirit, seen of angels, preached unto the Gentiles, believed on in the world, received up into glory.	Paul speaks here of the the mystery of godliness as being the secret shown to Him about the identity and nature of Jesus the Christ.
Rev 1:20	The <u>mystery</u> of the seven stars which thou sawest in my right hand, and the seven golden candlesticks. The seven stars are the angels of the seven churches: and the seven candlesticks which thou sawest are the seven churches.	The Mystery of the Seven Stars (Messengers)
Rev 10:7	But in the days of the voice of the seventh angel, when he shall begin to sound, the <u>mystery</u> of God should be finished, as he hath declared to his servants the prophets.	Here the phrase *mystery of God* is used to describe the conclusion of God's work in the world.

Rev 17:5	And upon her forehead *was* a name written, <u>MYSTERY</u>, BABYLON THE GREAT, THE MOTHER OF HARLOTS AND ABOMINATIONS OF THE EARTH.	The word mystery is used here in a title describing a false religious system inspired by Satan.
Rev 17:7	And the angel said unto me, Wherefore didst thou marvel? I will tell thee the <u>mystery</u> of the woman, and of the beast that carrieth her, which hath the seven heads and ten horns.	The angel tells John he will tell him the mystery about the woman representing the false religious system.

Limited Bibliography

Barry, John D., David Bomar, Derek R. Brown, Rachel Klippenstein, Douglas Mangum, Carrie Sinclair Wolcott, Lazarus Wentz, Elliot Ritzema, and Wendy Widder, eds. The Lexham Bible Dictionary. Bellingham, WA: Lexham Press, 2016.

Brand, Chad, Charles Draper, Archie England, Steve Bond, E. Ray Clendenen, Trent C. Butler, and Bill Latta, eds. Holman Illustrated Bible Dictionary. Nashville, TN: Holman Bible Publishers, 2003.

Cho, Youngmo. Spirit and Kingdom in the Writings of Luke and Paul: An Attempt to Reconcile These Concepts. Milton Keynes: Paternoster, 2005.

Day, A. Colin. Collins Thesaurus of the Bible. Bellingham, WA: Logos Bible Software, 2009.

Easton, M. G. Easton's Bible Dictionary. New York: Harper & Brothers, 1893.

Edersheim, Alfred. The Life and Times of Jesus the Messiah. Vol. 2. New York: Longmans, Green, and Co., 1896.

Edersheim, Alfred. The Temple, Its Ministry and Services as They Were at the Time of Jesus Christ. London: James Clarke & Co., 1959.

Elwell, Walter A., and Philip Wesley Comfort. Tyndale Bible Dictionary. Tyndale Reference Library. Wheaton, IL: Tyndale House Publishers, 2001.

Geisler, Norman L., and William E. Nix. A General Introduction to the Bible. Rev. and expanded. Chicago: Moody Press, 1986.

Jamieson, Robert, A. R. Fausset, and David Brown. *Commentary Critical and Explanatory on the Whole Bible.* Vol. 2 Oak Harbor, WA: Logos Research Systems, Inc., 1997

Lawrence, Brother, *The Practice of the Presence of God*, Digireads Publishing, 2016

Lightfoot, Joseph Barber, ed. Saint Paul's Epistle to the Philippians. Classic Commentaries on the Greek New Testament. London: Macmillan and Co., ltd, 1913.

Lightfoot, Joseph Barber, ed. St. Paul's Epistle to the Galatians. A Revised Text with Introduction, Notes, and Dissertations. 4th ed. Classic Commentaries on the Greek New Testament. London: Macmillan and Co., 1874.

MacArthur, John. The MacArthur Topical Bible: New King James Version. Nashville, TN: Word Publishing, 1999.

McGarvey, J. W. A Commentary on the Acts of the Apostles. Lexington, KY: Transylvania Printing and Publishing Co.,1872

Manser, Martin H. Dictionary of Bible Themes: The Accessible and Comprehensive Tool for Topical Studies. London: Martin Manser, 2009.

Mays, James Luther, ed. Harper's Bible Commentary. San Francisco: Harper & Row, 1988.

Milligan, George, ed. St. Paul's Epistles to the Thessalonians. Classic Commentaries on the Greek New Testament. London: Macmillan and Co., ltd, 1908.

Myers, Allen C. The Eerdmans Bible Dictionary. Grand Rapids, MI: Eerdmans, 1987.

Northrup, Bernard E. True Evangelism: Paul's Presentation of the First Five Steps of the Soul-Winner in Romans, 1997.

Ramsay, William Mitchell. St. Paul the Traveller and the Roman Citizen. London: Hodder & Stoughton, 1907.

Robertson, A. T. Paul the Interpreter of Christ. London: Hodder & Stoughton, 1921.

Smeaton, George. Paul's Doctrine of the Atonement : Taken from The Doctrine of the Atonement According to the Apostles. Simpsonville, SC: Christian Classics Foundation, 1996.

Smith, Stelman, and Judson Cornwall. The Exhaustive Dictionary of Bible Names. North Brunswick, NJ: Bridge-Logos, 1998.

Strong, James. A Concise Dictionary of the Words in the Greek Testament and The Hebrew Bible. Bellingham, WA: Logos Bible Software, 2009.

Strong, James. A Concise Dictionary of the Words in the Greek Testament and The Hebrew Bible. Bellingham, WA: Logos Bible Software, 2009.

Tanner, J. Paul. A Chronology of the Apostle Paul, 2nd Edition www.paultanner.org, 2003.

Utley, Robert James. Paul Bound, the Gospel Unbound: Letters from Prison (Colossians, Ephesians and Philemon, Then Later, Philippians). Vol. Volume 8. Study Guide Commentary Series. Marshall, TX: Bible Lessons International, 1997.

Utley, Robert James. Paul's First Letters: Galatians and I & II Thessalonians. Vol. Volume 11. Study

Guide Commentary Series. Marshall, TX: Bible Lessons International, 1997.

Utley, Robert James. Paul's Fourth Missionary Journey: I Timothy, Titus, II Timothy. Vol. Volume 9. Study Guide Commentary Series. Marshall, Texas: Bible Lessons International, 2000.

Utley, Robert James. Paul's Letters to a Troubled Church: I and II Corinthians. Vol. Volume 6. Study Guide Commentary Series. Marshall, TX: Bible Lessons International, 2002.

Utley, Robert James. The Gospel according to Paul: Romans. Vol. Volume 5. Study Guide Commentary Series. Marshall, Texas: Bible Lessons International, 1998.

Westcott, Brooke Foss, and John Maurice Schulhof, eds. Saint Paul's Epistle to the Ephesians: The Greek Text with Notes and Addenda. Classic Commentaries on the Greek New Testament. London; New York: The Macmillan Company, 1909.

Wuest, Kenneth S. Wuest's Word Studies from the Greek New Testament: For the English Reader. Grand Rapids: Eerdmans, 1997.

Youngblood, Ronald F., F. F. Bruce, and R. K. Harrison, Thomas Nelson Publishers, eds. Nelson's New Illustrated Bible Dictionary. Nashville, TN: Thomas Nelson, Inc., 1995.

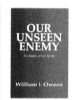

97806145R00163

Made in the USA
Columbia, SC
18 June 2018